RARE
CHARACTER DOLLS

RARE
CHARACTER DOLLS

Maree Tarnowska

Consultants
Richard Wright and Ralph Griffith

Introduction
Caroline G. Goodfellow

Hobby House Press, Inc.
Cumberland, Maryland 21502

FRONTISPIECE

The Jumeau boy doll in the Mardi
Gras costume is illustrated also on
page 73. The girl doll has the words
Tête Jumeau printed in red on its head.
The blue glass eyes are fixed, the
mouth is closed, and the ears are
applied. The doll is 25in (64cm) tall.
The lady-style, jointed body is of wood
and composition. The doll is not a
character doll although its costume
matches that of the accompanying boy
doll.

© Justin Knowles Ltd 1987

First published in the United States and
North America in 1987
by Hobby House Press Inc., 900 Frederick Street,
Cumberland, Maryland 21502.
(301) 759-3770.

ISBN: 0 87588 306 0

Produced by the Justin Knowles Publishing Group,
9 Colleton Crescent, Exeter, Devon, England

Design: Vic Giolitto

Typeset by Keyspools Ltd, Warrington

Printed and bound in Hong Kong by
Mandarin Offset Ltd

First American Edition.

Contents

Incised *Bru Jne. 7*, this oriental-type doll is 20in (51cm) tall. The fixed glass eyes are brown, and the mouth is closed. The entire doll, including the leather body, bisque head, bisque lower arms and wooden lower legs, is a pale coffee colour, while the black, slanting eyebrows and Japanese-style wig add to the oriental effect.

The small doll, which is 8in (20cm) tall, bears the incised figure *19*. Made by Simon & Halbig, it is all bisque and has glass eyes.

Foreword

At the top end of the doll collecting market French *bébés* have long held a secure position, enjoying pride of place in the collections of many enthusiasts worldwide alongside early wood, wax and fashion dolls. The ubiquitous baby doll, produced in much greater numbers by such doll makers as Armand Marseille and Simon & Halbig, together with the more adult and fully jointed items from the same companies, often form only a small part of such collections. That this is so might be because novice collectors sometimes lack the confidence to make their first purchases from among the rare and more expensive dolls.

Yet most collections, if they reflect the desire of the owner to display examples from the whole range of antique dolls, will often contain a few character dolls, that is, dolls that have facial features that more closely represent those of a human child or adult than the stylized and beautified faces found on most other types of doll. These "pretty" dolls represent what the doll makers of the past believed was the ultimate in feminine beauty; the character dolls were an attempt to represent the human face with more truth and realism, the results ranging from a recognizable normality to a carefree caricature.

The general production of character dolls, with few exceptions, did not commence until the end of the 19th century. Before that time such dolls were mainly confined to those that were intended to be lifelike represent-ations of particular people, often aristocrats or those famous enough to merit the special attention of the public at large. The production of the bisque-head character doll, with which this book is concerned, was confined to a relatively short period of time: not much more than the first two decades of the 20th century. Like many other things, the outbreak of World War I led to a temporary halt in supplies from the main producer, Germany, after which the renewal of trade was a faltering process that never reached its pre-war peak before being overtaken by new styles, materials, designs and competition from other sources. It is therefore hardly surprising that the output of character dolls never reached the volume attained by the more stylized dolls, which, of course, continued to be produced for the whole of this period.

The move to greater realism in the visual appearance of dolls was assisted by a determined effort on the part of those who were involved to bring this about. In an exhibition at Munich in 1908 there was much emphasis on "doll reform" and one of the participants was Marion Kaulitz who, in common with others, used the term "art dolls" to describe the dolls that we now know as character dolls. In 1911 Schoenhut used the same term for the all-wood character dolls that were produced in the United States by that company.

The pressures for a general production of these dolls must have been increased by these events. In this context, the words "doll reform" meant a move to convince the doll makers that there was a need to produce more human-looking faces for their dolls and, believing this, the doll makers issued the necessary orders to their staff.

In the race that followed the artists responsible for designing the heads for the dolls might well have been swept away by a new-found freedom to make use of their artistic talents and have produced a plethora of original designs. We know, however, that many examples of character heads were based on the faces of the children and grandchildren of the doll makers, and there would, therefore, have been many, many models available for this purpose. But supply must always be coupled with demand, and if every original had been produced on a mass scale, which was well within the capability of the major manufacturers, the supply would soon have outstripped the marketing potential. It seems reasonable to assume that some moulds were used for a comparatively short run before being replaced by another.

It must also be remembered that when it first appeared the character doll was a relatively new concept as a child's plaything and was in direct competition with the attractions of the long-established conventional doll. The more natural look of the new doll, which, in some cases, displayed many of the less-attractive grimaces of a petulant child, might not have had an immediate appeal to the romantic and fairytale notions of a young child of those times. Adults might have been amused by such dolls and bought them for their offspring. But they may not have represented the first choice of the child itself, although they would, undoubtedly, have been received with dutiful acknowledgement by the acquiescent daughter of that era.

So the emergence of the true character doll during the first decade of the 20th century was not a trouble free occurrence. The public was not immediately enraptured, and its loyalty to the traditional presentation of female beauty remained strong. It has even been recorded that some editions of the new-type doll proved such poor "sellers" that the manufacturers were left with no option but to destroy those remaining unsold. It has even been suggested that the character dolls appeared before their time! This is in stark contrast to the interest and enthusiasm that the collectors of today display.

All this should help to explain the title of this book – *Rare Character Dolls*. They are rare from a combination of circumstances. The limited period during which they were produced; the mass of original designs which, in some cases, resulted in smaller numbers of certain editions being offered for sale; and their more restricted sales appeal, all combined to reduce the number of such dolls that would be available for posterity. In addition of course, to these reasons must be added the occasional mishap common to all bisque-head dolls when fragile heads came into violent contact with unyielding nursery floors.

Even today it is doubtful if the total range of these dolls has been discovered and documented, and it would be surprising if further examples did not re-emerge in the future. Certain editions have been seen, and owned, by collectors everywhere, but there are also many others that, for whatever reason, remain outside the experience of most enthusiasts. It is on these that this book concentrates.

When it was first suggested that collectors might be interested in a book that illustrated and included details of these dolls, it was realized that to find sufficient and varied items might be a Herculean task involving time and travel far beyond the shores of the United Kingdom. The location of a few suitable examples was known, and further enquiries produced information regarding one or two more. As time passed the search widened and then, quite suddenly, fortune smiled. It was obvious that the United States, with its long and firmly established interest in antique dolls, might offer the best chance of finding suitable items. It was there that, contained in two major collections, some very fine examples of character dolls were found, and these, together with a smaller number from other sources, are illustrated in this book.

It is not suggested that every doll illustrated on the pages that follow can claim the same degree of rarity. Some have been included that collectors will recognize from past experience, but even these are by no means common and are worth including in the interests of giving a more complete picture of this fascinating group of dolls. It will also be noted that the character dolls illustrated and described in this book are entirely bisque-head examples. This is not because those made of other materials are never designated as "rare" but rather because of the greater interest that has been shown by today's collectors in the bisque-head type, an interest supported by the very high prices that these dolls reach at auction.

It is also interesting to note that certain of these dolls have appeared in the pages of price guides, but generally without an indication of their cash value. The explanation for this is that no example of the doll has been sold in the recent past and its value cannot therefore be realistically assessed. This is a further indication of a rare doll.

Maree Tarnowska

Introduction

It may be said that all dolls are character dolls. Certainly, to their owners, all dolls have that little "something" that sets them apart from all the others. Many dolls were also given a name, either by their makers or by their owners, and these names have tended to follow closely those popular at any particular time.

Until recent times, when mechanical devices have been employed to paint facial features to a uniform, multi-thousand standard, the features of a doll's face were painted by hand. Each manufacturer had a particular style of painting – feathered eyebrows, mouth lines, the colours used and so forth. However, as each doll was painted individually, each one is individual within the limits of the standards set by the manufacturer.

Throughout the last three hundred years, the type of doll that was made has followed the fashion dictates of the day, whether they decreed that lady, baby or child dolls should be produced. The faces and bodies of the dolls were designed to follow the style and shape desired at any given time, and these changed many times – not always has the slender, long-legged girl doll been most popular.

At the same time, manufacturers were experimenting with all sorts of methods to enhance the natural appearance of their dolls. When the more or less rigid fashion dolls were in vogue, the shape was fairly simple, but if a child or baby doll was required, adaptations became necessary and were often very sophisticated. It was not lifelike for a baby doll to have an adult's face or shape. Doll manufacturers began to design faces that were based on real people. Children, often from the makers' families, were the models, copied at their best and worst. When Kämmer & Reinhardt introduced the first named character dolls in 1909, the dolls were modelled on the grandchildren of the owners of the company. About the same time, Käthe Kruse used her own children as models, and Gebrüder Heubach took the idea further with both dolls and figurines. Most of these 20th-century dolls were shaped as babies and young children, whose wealth of expressions varied greatly. Few lady dolls were made as character dolls, mainly because fashion demands standardization rather than individuality.

Dolls' heads, in general, are made of wood, wax, glazed china, bisque, cloth or plastic. The first three of these materials were rarely used to create what are now known as character dolls – although some of the early dolls made from these materials are certainly individual – mainly because the

The final assembly and packing room at Kämmer & Reinhardt's Waltershausen factory.

concepts had not been thought of nor the necessary technical standards reached at the time these materials were commonly used. The material most widely used for dolls' heads was unglazed porcelain, which is known as bisque. By the time bisque became popular with doll manufacturers, not only had the techniques of casting it and designing the moulds been perfected, but also the desire to attain the expressive rather than the simply pretty face had reached a point where "character" faces could be both successfully made and generally appreciated. Even so, fewer character dolls were produced than the ever-popular pretty-faced dolls.

Cloth is a very specialist material in the making of dolls. It is extremely costly to use as it requires a great deal of individual attention to create a face at all. Hand painting and special treatments to retain the colour and surface of the cloth have to be employed, as do careful modelling and moulding techniques.

Wood, which has been used to make dolls from the earliest times, was rarely used for creating character faces. Very occasionally a maker attempted to produce a character doll, with some rather staggering results, for the faces were often coupled with unusual body types.

The new plastic materials that appeared in the late 19th century, on the

Glass eyes being matched and inserted into bisque dolls' heads.

other hand, could be readily used for character faces as they were moulded. Celluloid, which was introduced at the end of the 19th century, was the most common of the plastic materials. The main difference between plastic and bisque was cost: plastic dolls were cheaper to produce. However, plastic tends to become discolored, and it can easily be damaged by fire or by being stepped on or dropped.

As with the human face, the most important focal point of a doll's face is the eyes, and the placement of the eyes can profoundly alter the doll's physical appearance and expression, a slight mis-alignment producing faces that no one likes. One of the major advances in doll making during the 19th century was the development of the "sleeping" eye mechanism, an essential refinement when baby dolls were introduced. It is not realistic for a baby doll to appear to be sleeping when its eyes remain open, staring orbs; on the other hand, dolls with permanently closed eyes appear to be dead.

Early in the 19th century, "sleeping" eyes were developed which had to be moved by hand, by pushing or pulling a wire that was attached to the eyes, ran through the body and protruded at the waist or hip line. Later, the wire was shortened and a lead weight added to its base so that it hung down within the head. When the doll was laid down, the weight shifted toward

The doll assembly room.

the back of the head, drawing the eyes with it so that they moved down and appeared shut. Sometimes, the method was adapted so that only the eyelids moved over static eyes.

Blown glass, either blue or brown, was used for the eyes themselves. During the early 20th century, makers introduced intaglio eyes, which were moulded with concave irises and pupils. An integral part of the face, intaglio eyes were hand painted and highlighted. The greatest exponent of this art was the firm of Gebrüder Heubach.

The treatment of a doll's eyebrows and lashes can also alter the expression of its face, making it appear to be happy, sad or cross.

When character dolls became popular, makers had the opportunity to use another type of eye – the side-glancing eye – to great effectiveness. "Flirting" eyes is the term used now to describe eyes that actually move from side to side. Such eyes were used in dolls as early as the mid-19th century, although few of these eyes closed as well. At the beginning of the 20th century, many patents were obtained for eyes that moved both vertically and horizontally, by using both eye and eyelid movement. Carl Halbig, of Simon & Halbig, obtained such a patent in 1904, and its idea of a single weight movement may have been used in the Kämmer & Reinhardt/ Simon & Halbig doll The Flirt, which was issued in 1908 as part of the Royal dolls line.

The skilled task of painting dolls' heads and making eyelashes.

Eyes that glance to the side without moving from side to side are referred to as "roguish" eyes. These eyes were popular too, especially during this century and with American doll designers and makers. Dolls known as googly-eyed have this side-glancing feature, which can make a doll's face appear happy or sad, but very often mischievous.

Some dolls with roguish eyes have other facial characteristics that enhance the mischievous looks their designers or makers were attempting to create. The eyebrows are often painted quite high on the forehead, or they are simple straight, upward-tilted lines; the nose is often a "button" type; and the mouth is often a single lip, almost semi-circular in shape set either straight on or slightly up and to the side (usually to the side to which the eyes are glancing). Such mouths are sometimes called "water melon" or "water melon slice" mouths because only the lower lip shows and the arc is so distinct.

The treatment of the lower face, in particular the mouth, can also affect the look of a doll. Giving dolls open mouths, with or without teeth and a tongue, was another way in which manufacturers sought to make their dolls realistic. After trials with a double row of teeth, which tended to give a grimace-like look, most manufacturers opted for either a top or a bottom row of teeth. The smiling, open mouths, with either moulded teeth or set-in teeth, were most popular when they were produced, but these are not

Dolls' bodies receiving a first coat of paint.

necessarily the ones most sought after today by collectors who seek the unusual. Makers of character dolls used all the styles of mouth available to them to create the happy baby, the child with dimples, the screaming child, the cheeky child or the solemn child. All are quite different, and all are appealing in their own ways.

As well as the heads and faces, the dolls' bodies were being constantly changed, both in their design and the material used. The solid, wooden blocks, partly turned to give a semblance of human shape, gave way to soft cloth bodies. The straight wooden legs and strange wood, cloth or kid half-arms became cloth upper arms and thighs, with moulded wax or china lower legs and arms with hands. As most dolls were dressed in garments reaching to the lower legs and, with babies, beyond the feet, it was not necessary to use the costly moulded materials for those parts of the body that remained unseen. The greatest advantage of the moulded substances – bisque and plastic – was the delicate casting and modelling that could be achieved. Hands and fingers, feet and toes could be well defined, even to the extent of having nails, knuckles and dimples. Generally, the hands and feet were proportionately smaller than the heads.

Kid, a very fine leather, was used as body material, achieving great popularity for the French fashion dolls made from 1860 to 1880. As with

the wooden bodies, kid bodies were carefully shaped, but they were sewn and stuffed to give the ideal shape sought after by ladies of the time. It is not possible to create a doll's shape by corsetry as a real person might; it must be done with the construction of the doll's body itself.

Towards the end of the 19th century, as manufacturers continued to strive after realism, more dolls were created that could take up a variety of positions – standing, sitting and kneeling, their arms up, down or bent. A substance already being used for making dolls' heads was employed for bodies and limbs; its name, composition. This is a papier mâché-like material based on wood or paper pulp with glues and other additives that made it strong yet light. As it could be moulded, composition was increasingly used for bodies and limbs. It could also be designed to be jointed at the major points – neck, shoulders and hips – with additional jointing, when desired, at the elbows, wrists, waist, knees and ankles. Dolls can be found with all combinations of jointing.

Body shapes could also be moulded in composition, and very effectively too. Lady dolls with rounded busts and hips, narrow waists and shapely legs were made; child dolls with straight bodies and legs were created, and baby dolls with rounded bodies, often quite pot-bellied, were designed with special chubby limbs in a curved, almost semi-circular shape. Known

Dolls' arms were formed by being punched out of composition, one by one, before being taken on trays to the assembly room.

17

as "bent-limb" baby dolls, the toes and fingers of these dolls look very lifelike.

Not all dolls made between 1880 and 1940 had composition bodies, but the majority did, and such bodies were made by specialists working to the requirements of the manufacturers of the dolls' heads. Some makers opted for individually designed bodies to match their own head designs. This was especially true of such makers as Käthe Kruse, who designed both heads and bodies to produce an overall effect of size, weight and conformity of appearance. Her baby dolls, in fact, looked, felt and weighed as a real child might, with the appropriate floppiness of the head and body when the doll was picked up.

Most dolls were assembled before being exported, although they were not always dressed. However, sometimes heads, limbs and bodies were sent separately as a way around import tax and duty regulations. Thus sprang up, especially in the United States, many importers who also assembled dolls before distributing them or who imported heads only while the bodies were made by American companies. Occasionally some American importers designed heads themselves, which were then manufactured on their behalf in Germany. In such cases, the American company retained the copyright to the doll, and it may have employed a number of manufacturers to create the dolls or dolls' heads. The influence of the American market during the early years of this century increased dramatically as the country became the largest importer of dolls. It was only during the years 1914 to 1918, when German stocks were withdrawn because of World War I, that the importers turned to and developed makers in their own country and in Japan.

The American Influence

Several of the American importers and distributors of dolls that became established during the late 19th century or early 20th century are still in business today. Some of these companies are now among the largest in the world, continuing to supply dolls of all types as they have done for more than fifty years. Often through these companies, the talents of many other individuals – designers, painters and sculptors – were developed.

New York City became the centre of the doll trade in all its various aspects – importation, distribution and manufacturing. Those companies established there which now remain, still retain their New York head-quarters, although some of the more recently founded have headquarters in other cities such as Mattel, which is near Los Angeles in California.

The **Acme Toy Manufacturing Company** was established in New York City in 1908 and produced good quality composition dolls, both baby dolls and the "talking" mama dolls. In 1914 its range included a group of unbreakable character dolls, which was added to and changed over a number of years. The company used the simple trademark *Acme Toy Co.* In 1925 Acme was sued by E. I. Horsman & Co. for copying the Tinie Baby doll (page 57), but Horsman lost the case as the doll was not marked with the company's full name but only with the initials *EIH*.

Louis Amberg & Son was founded in 1878 in Cincinnati, Ohio, and

LA&S
RA 241 5/0
GERMANY

GERMANY
A-R
LA&S 886.2

twenty years later the company moved to New York City. Amberg imported dolls from Germany, but in 1910 it became one of the first to manufacture on a large scale dolls completely made in the United States. Over the years, Amberg developed hundreds of different dolls, many of them named character dolls. The company employed artists and designers, including Grace G. Drayton and Jeno Juszko, who contributed to the range of seventy-five dolls, collectively known as Baby Beautiful, which was issued from 1910. Juszko also designed for Amberg the New Born Babe which represented a two-day-old infant, and which was first issued in 1914.

Otto Ernst Denivelle was another of those who worked closely with Amberg, and he not only supervised the manufacture of Amberg's dolls but also designed new dolls and new methods of production. Denivelle also worked for other American companies including Horsman and Effanbee. Around 1910, he worked with his brother to improve the manufacture of the cold-press composition used for making dolls' heads by introducing collapsible moulds, a technique that helped to overcome the distortion that tended to occur during the drying process. Joseph Kallus worked for the brothers during his student days. As well as the practical side of manufacturing, Denivelle also held a few copyrights for dolls, including the patented design for Sunny Orange Blossom (1924), one of the dolls distributed by Amberg. The marks sometimes found on Denivelle dolls are the initials *Deco*, often within an ellipse.

The idea of distributing in the United States the best of the dolls manufactured in Europe appealed to George Borgfeldt, and in 1881 he founded a company with that aim in mind. **George Borgfeldt & Company** grew rapidly from its base in New York City to become the largest distributor of dolls, and the company had offices in many towns, both in the United States and in Europe. Besides being a distributor, the company had many dolls made exclusively to its own specifications, and American manufacturers were added to its long list of German and Japanese suppliers.

Many of the Borgfeldt dolls were designed by artists such as Joseph Kallus and made by an appointed company, Borgfeldt retaining the copyrights. Possibly the most famous of these was Kewpie, created as a doll by Kallus from Rose O'Neill's drawings.

Many doll making companies produced dolls solely for Borgfeldt. Among these was the K. & K. Toy Company, which was founded in 1915. The initials (although advertised as "K and K means Kept Klean") probably stood for Kolb and Kahle, the partners of Borgfeldt himself. About 1926, the K. & K. Toy Company was absorbed by the Cameo Doll Company.

In 1926, the American doll designer Joseph Kallus copyrighted the tradename *Baby Bo-Kaye* (page 36). This is a cloth-bodied doll with composition arms and legs. The heads for this doll could be made of bisque, composition or celluloid, and they were manufactured in both Germany and the United States. The bisque heads were usually made by Alt, Beck & Gottschalck, while the celluloid ones were supplied by Rheinische Gummi-

G.327 JB
Germany
A 10 M

251
G.B
Germany
A 2/0 M
D.R.G.M
243/1

und Celluloid-Fabrik, both German companies. The composition heads were made in America by the Cameo Doll Company. The style of the heads was always the same: short, moulded hair with a slight side parting swept gently to the left, an open mouth with two lower teeth and "sleeping" glass eyes.

Only the heads of the Baby Bo-Kaye dolls were imported. The dolls were assembled by the body makers, K. & K. Toy Co., on behalf of Borgfeldt, which distributed the dolls. It is possible that the "Bo" in the name stands for Borgfeldt, while the "Kaye" represents Kallus. Baby Bo-Kaye was also one of the names registered by Borgfelt as a trademark in Germany.

Butler Brothers was a mail-order company founded in 1877 in New York City and at Sonneberg, and establishing subsidiary offices in the United States over the years. As importers, wholesalers and distributors, the company handled all types of dolls – glazed china, bisque, composition and celluloid – and advertised European as well as American dolls. The majority of these advertised dolls had tradenames, often representing specific types such as nations, costumes or occupations – Russian Princess, Banker's Daughter, for example – while others were novelty dolls such as Santa Claus. The company also distributed accessories for dolls such as tea sets and clothing.

The company **Fleischaker & Baum** was established in New York City in 1910 and is still a major doll making concern, trading today under the name of its original trademark *Effanbee*. The company opened a factory to produce composition dolls and manufactured many hundreds of different types, including characters, babies and children, mama dolls and dolls with roguish eyes. In 1919 Effanbee used the statement "They Walk, They Talk, They Sleep" to describe the mama dolls that became very popular in Britain. Most of the large distributors, shops and mail-order businesses sold Effanbee dolls, and the dolls were widely exported.

Many of the popular early Effanbee dolls were re-issued; these included Baby Dainty (1912) and Baby Grumpy (1914). One of the most popular and long-lasting dolls was Patsy, originally registered in 1927. Many versions of this doll were issued under different names, and its body type, with a reverse socket neck, became standard for many Effanbee dolls of the 1930s.

Effanbee made both all-composition bodies and cloth bodies with composition or cloth limbs. The dolls had "sleeping" eyes, although these were more often of metal and celluloid than of glass.

Baby Grumpy was a tradename registered by Effanbee in 1914, and the production of the doll continued until the 1940s. It was distributed by Butler Brothers, Carson, Pirie, Scott & Company (a Chicago store selling a large range of American and European dolls including Dolly Mine (1914) and Fairy Doll (1911)), and other stores including Marshall Field and Gimbel Brothers. In 1927, a smaller version, Grumpykins, was introduced. The doll's face has down-turned eyes below a frowning forehead, as if it is ready to burst into tears, and a rather pursed mouth. The hair is moulded into thickish curls around the face, and a large curl cascades down the forehead. The early dolls have cloth bodies with composition limbs; later versions have all-composition bodies. A 1927 advertisement for Grumpykins gave a wonderful but dramatic description of the "cute little doll with a bit of a frown [which] portrays a passing shadow," and it went on to say: "Our sculptor has caught the baby in a passing moment of petulancy, with a result that is electric in its appeal. Every mother will see her child in Grumpykins." Both black and white versions of the doll were made, and marks for Otto Ernst Denivelle have been found on them. Gebrüder Hcubach also made a similar figurine, and it may be that one was a copy of the other, although which was the copy is impossible to determine.

Edward Imerson Horsman established his business in 1865 in New York City. He started as a toy distributor, gradually adding to his range during the 1870s dolls that were assembled in the United States from parts imported from Germany. One of his main interests were rag dolls or those such as Billikins that were made partially of rag as well as others based on Teddy Bears. By 1919, Horsman had secured control of the Can't Break 'Em dolls distributed by Borgfeldt. Using designs by a number of artists, including Grace G. Drayton, Helen Trowbridge and Bernard Lipfert, Horsman introduced character dolls such as the Campbell Kids in 1910 and the HEbees-SHEbees, based on drawings by Charles Twelvetrees, in 1925.

The Aetna Doll and Toy Company was founded as the Aetna Toy Animal Company in 1907, and the name was changed a year later when the company acquired the rights for the Can't Break 'Em dolls. It amalgamated with Horsman in 1919.

From 1910 Horsman made the Campbell Kids (page 133) under licence from the Joseph Campbell Company, the soup makers, which owned the drawings. Horsman used the composition Can't Break 'Em heads, and various styles were designed and added to. The first Campbell Kids were a boy and girl dressed in individually designed costumes. They have smiling faces, short bobbed hair, either moulded or as wigs, and moulded and painted eyes glancing to the side (the type known as roguish eyes). The early bodies are of cloth, sometimes jointed at the shoulders, hips and knees, with composition lower arms and legs. The later dolls are also made of all composition. The Campbell Kids family of dolls were very popular and relatively inexpensive.

Joseph L. Kallus of Brooklyn, New York, was one of the best known of all American doll designers and manufacturers. Beginning his career with George Borgfeldt when he was still a student at the Pratt Institute in 1912, Kallus was introduced to Rose O'Neill and translated her drawings of the Kewpies into three dimensions. By 1916, Kallus had founded the Rex Doll Company, which for two years produced wood-pulp composition dolls, mainly Kewpies, for Borgfeldt. Many of these Kewpies were distributed to the "carnival" trade by the Tip Top Toy Company of New York (1912–21).

Baby Bundie (1918) was the first of many dolls for which Kallus obtained the copyright, and while he was with the Mutual Doll Company (1919–21) he added the child doll Bo-Fair (1920); the baby doll Dollie (1920); a character doll, Lassie (1921); and Vanitie, a Spanish lady character doll (1921). Kallus resigned from the Mutual Doll Company to start the Cameo

© 1924
E.I. HORSMAN INC.
Made in
Germany

©
E.I.H. CO. INC.

Copr. by
J.L. Kallus
Germany
1394/30

Doll Company, which made both composition and fabric (embossed buckram) dolls' heads with composition, wood or fabric bodies. He added to his list of copyrights many dolls and patents for construction, leg movements and joints, including the segmented doll's body made of eighteen parts. Most of his dolls were designed with moulded hairstyles.

The list of Kallus-designed dolls is very large and covers most of the very popular models of the 1920s and 1930s. Many were character dolls, and they include Baby Bundie; Baby Bo-Kaye (page 36); Little Annie Rooney, designed from the cartoon drawings by Jack Collins (1925); Baby Blossom, a small child character doll (1927); Canyon Country Kiddies, taken from drawings by James Swinnerton (1927); Bozo, a humanized dog, and Sissie, a smiling child (1928); Margie (1929), a smiling child and the first doll to have an eighteen-part body; and Scootles (1930s).

During the 1930s, Kallus designed both advertising dolls and those based on the new movie and radio stars. Among the first group were RCA Radiotron Doll (1930); Drum Major, later known as Band Master and shortened to Bandy, designed for General Electric (1935); Koppers Koke (1933); Hotpoint; Mr Peanut and Conmar Major, which advertised zippers. Among the cartoon, movie and radio celebrities were Betty Boop (1932), originally designed by Fleischer Studios for Paramount Pictures; Popeye, a 1932 creation made under licence from King Features; Baby Snooks (1939), which was actually made by the Ideal Novelty & Toy Company from a Kallus design representing Fanny Brice in the rôle; and Pinocchio (1939), from the Walt Disney cartoon character, which was also made by Ideal Novelty & Toy Co.

The Bye-lo Baby was designed by **Grace Storey Putnam** in 1922, and it was described as: "life size modelled from a baby three days old." Borgfeldt was the only licensee for the doll, but both the heads and the bodies were made by a number of companies in both Germany and America. It was also copied, while it may itself have been a copy of the New Born Babe produced by Amberg in 1914. The heads came as bisque, wax or composition with a flange neck and cloth body, which was designed by Georgene Averill. All-bisque versions were also issued, as were dolls with rubber heads. Later, vinyl versions were manufactured.

Founded in Philadelphia in 1872, **A. Schoenhut & Co.** made all-wood dolls and toys such as the Humpty Dumpty Circus. The dolls – called "All Wood Perfection Art Dolls" – had carved wooden heads with moulded hairstyles and fully jointed wooden bodies, which could be positioned easily, for the joints were metal springs and the feet were drilled with holes to fit onto a small stand.

F.A.O. Schwarz was one of four brothers from Germany who opened large toyshops in various American towns and cities. Between them, the brothers controlled many lines, but F.A.O. Schwarz dealt generally with German products rather than French or English ones. Among this toyshop's range were dolls by Simon & Halbig, Kämmer & Reinhardt and Kestner. F.A.O. Schwarz's New York shop was established in 1862, and it still commands a Fifth Avenue corner site near Central Park, selling dolls and toys from the cheapest to the most expensive and exclusive. The

company also sold American dolls including the Tinie Baby made by Horsman (page 57).

Strobel & Wilken Co. began as a toy importer in Cincinnati, Ohio, in 1864 and later moved to New York City, adding dolls to its range. The company distributed both American and European dolls of various materials, including bisque, rag and celluloid. Also in its range were the American Beauty (1895), and the Kämmer & Reinhardt Royal dolls, which were issued from 1903, and it eventually included the Flirt (1908) and, from 1909, Kämmer & Reinhardt character dolls. Between 1910 and 1924, Strobel & Wilken advertised many new lines of character dolls together with dolls made by Ideal Novelty & Toy Co., American Art dolls and others.

German Manufacturers

For more than four hundred years, Germany provided the world with its toys including dolls. As changes occurred in the "real" world, so they were reflected in the toys, as were changes and developments in the methods and processes of the manufacture. Wooden dolls had always been made, but with the development of the porcelain factories, tremendous advances took place throughout the entire doll manufacturing world. At first dolls' heads and parts were made by established companies from material left over after the dinner services, figurines and ornaments had been created. Other companies produced heads on behalf of a second company as a strict business venture, as porcelain factories are commissioned to work today. Gradually, however, new factories, producing only dolls' heads and parts, were established.

The main German porcelain factories were situated in the area known as Thüringia, just to the north of Bavaria, and many of the factories were in or near Waltershausen and Ohrdruf. The chain of manufacture and distribution was well established by the time porcelain dolls began to be made, and areas already producing composition, wood and rag items simply added dolls to their lists. For example, the principle region for the production of composition was around Sonneberg and the small town of Neustadt bei Coburg, and composition dolls' bodies and parts were generally made there. As Sonneberg was the main wholesale town from which the toys had been exported, it retained this rôle for dolls too.

Among the best known of the German manufacturers of bisque dolls and character dolls was Simon & Halbig, which worked in conjunction with Kämmer & Reinhardt, Kestner, Gebrüder Heubach and Armand Marseille. Between them, these companies produced millions of dolls in hundreds of different styles and types – lady dolls, child dolls and baby dolls – for more than forty years. Their dolls were exported around the world. As well as making dolls from their own designs, they made dolls to the specifications of other companies or designers, often for the major American distributors.

The firm of **Alt, Beck & Gottschalck** was established in 1854 at Nauendorf, near Ohrdruf. It is thought now that the company made many of the late 19th-century glazed china and bisque heads that had elaborate

1362
Made in Germany
3

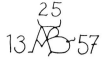

1100

Catterfelder Puppenfabrik

2

152
L.W. & Co
12

moulded hairstyles. After 1910, the company introduced a range of character dolls with mould numbers in the 1300s. The mould *1322* doll (page 36) is a later version of a mould designed as a happy smiling boy character doll with intaglio eyes, an open mouth showing two upper teeth and a tongue, and dimples. When glass eyes were introduced to the mould, they could be either "sleeping" or fixed. Heads marked *1322* have been found on bent-limb bodies as well as on toddler bodies. Latterly, Alt, Beck & Gottschalck produced bisque heads for Borgfeldt, including, in the 1920s, the Bye-lo Baby.

Bähr & Pröschild was established at Ohrdruf in 1871 as a porcelain factory making china dolls, heads and bathing dolls. By 1910, the company was also making dolls' parts and, later, celluloid heads. Many Bähr & Pröschild doll heads were used by other companies, including Bruno Schmidt of Waltershausen, which acquired the factory in 1918 (page 39).

Catterfelder Puppenfabrik was established in 1906 at Catterfeld near Waltershausen. The company produced porcelain dolls, making both heads and parts as well as using heads made by other companies. Its main stock was character dolls, babies and child dolls together with some semi-mechanical figures. Among their best known tradenames are My Sunshine (*Mein Sonnenschein*, 1910), and Little Sunshine (*Kleiner Sonnenschein*, 1922) (page 122).

Eisenmann & Company was established in 1881 in Fürth, Bavaria, and later in London. This company made and distributed a wide range of dolls and toys including rag dolls, the most famous of which were known as the London Rag Dolls. Many of the company's named character dolls were actually registered in England. Eisenmann & Co. used the initials *Einco* as its trademark. Generally, when the company used bisque heads, these were produced by Gebrüder Heubach (page 44).

In 1879 **William Goebel** took over the porcelain factory founded by his father in 1871 at Oeslau, Bavaria. This company still makes dolls and figurines, the most famous of which are the Hummel figures. By 1900, the factory was making only figures, dolls and heads, in both glazed china and bisque, and many of the heads were produced for other makers. Usually, the company's marks showed an entwined *W* and *G* below a simplified crown shape.

Hertel, Schwab & Co. was established at the Stutzhauser Porzellanfabrik near Ohrdruf in 1910. As makers of both glazed china and bisque doll heads and all-bisque dolls, the company produced mainly character heads, many of which were used by other companies such as Kley & Hahn, König & Wernicke and Strobel & Wilken. For Borgfeldt, the company produced heads for the Bye-lo Baby. The company's mould number *173* was created for Strobel & Wilken. The face of the doll was that of a child with roguish eyes, and the head can be found on both bent-limb bodies and on the straight-limbed toddler bodies. Mould number *163*, also made for Strobel & Wilken, represented an older child with a moulded side-parting hairstyle. This doll's face had the common "water melon slice" smiling mouth often found on dolls with roguish eyes (pages 44 and 45).

The **Gebrüder Heubach** porcelain factory was founded in 1840 in

Lichte near Wallendorf, Thüringia, and later in Sonneberg. It made some of the first and most unusual of all the character dolls and heads and also modelled figurines using similar facial expressions. The dolls were widely exported, and their most notable features were the intaglio eyes, which were incised in the moulding before being, painted and highlighted. Unfortunately, the composition bodies made or used by the company were of poorer quality than the heads, but they do not detract from the superb heads themselves. Gebrüder Heubach used two distinct marks, one a rising sun design and the other a square containing the letters *HEUBACH*. The rising sun mark was registered in 1882, but the later square mark is more frequently found. Heubach supplied heads for other companies, possibly even Jumeau (pages 46–55).

In 1886 a company was founded at Waltershausen by a designer and modeller, Ernst Kämmer, and a business man, Franz Reinhardt. This new company, named **Kämmer & Reinhardt**, acted as a *Verleger*, a German term that now translates as publisher. That is to say, the company controlled the production and assembly of dolls' heads, bodies and parts without actually manufacturing the individual components. Kämmer & Reinhardt did design many of the dolls, and the company held the copyrights and patents for its dolls, including the character dolls registered in 1909. In addition to organizing the manufacture of its own dolls, the company also arranged for specific dolls to be made for individual distributors, such as the Favorite line for F.A.O. Schwarz.

The company's trademark was *K. & R.* with the *&* contained within a six-pointed star. Between 1900 and 1909, Kämmer & Reinhardt copyrighted several dolls – *Mein Liebling*, Majestic, Royal, *Die Kokette*, The Flirt, *Der Schelm* and others – and then, in 1909, it registered *Charakterpuppen*, and so began a long line of named dolls, from babies to older children, both boys and girls, with a wide range of facial expression, and a group of comic figures.

Kämmer & Reinhardt was a prolific producer of dolls, and many of the company's designs were translated into bisque by one of the best of the manufacturers of bisque heads, Simon & Halbig, and into celluloid by the Rheinische Gummi- und Celluloid-Fabrik. As well as bisque and celluloid, the company handled composition, rubber, wood, wax and felt dolls. It arranged the production of and advertised a huge range of different dolls: there were walking and talking dolls, dolls based on comic and literary characters, baby, child and lady dolls, the "normal" pretty-faced dolls; and dolls representing occupations, professions and trades, including soldiers and sailors. All these were in addition to the *Charakterpuppen*.

Mould number *114*, which was designed by Kämmer & Reinhardt and manufactured by Simon & Halbig, was part of the *Charakterpuppen* range that was introduced in 1909. The mould represents a child, and it has either glass or painted eyes and a closed mouth, and it has either a wig or flock hair. This mould number was given the tradenames Hans or Gretchen, the sex depending largely on the wig supplied, and it was said that the grandchildren of Franz Reinhardt were the models for the designs and that the two names were theirs. Exported throughout the world, mould

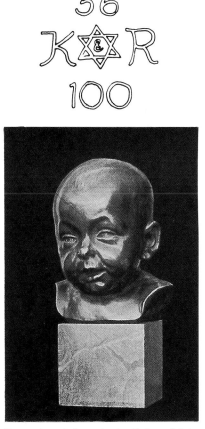

Reproduced above is the *Origanalbüste des Babykopfes* (the original of the Baby doll's head), the first of Kämmer & Reinhardt's character dolls.

In the booklet published to celebrate its first twenty-five years, Kämmer & Reinhardt described how it came to produce character dolls: "At the Munich exhibition in the summer of 1908, there was a group of so-called 'artist dolls', which, justifiably, created a stir as they promised something completely new. The idea of manufacturing these dolls originated with artists in Munich who maintained that the old dolls' heads were stereotyped and, because of their unnatural idealization, trite. … We inspected [these new dolls] closely and came to the conclusion that their success … was primarily achieved through the artistic arrangement and colour of the clothes. When we studied them in detail, we found that most of these heads were ugly…. Nevertheless, we did not underestimate the significance of the new trend … and decided to continue along the road taken by the Munich artists. We turned therefore to a specially recommended Berlin artist, and after thorough discussion he showed us a bronze bust, made by himself, of the head of a child about six weeks old, which he recommended that we use for the manufacture of dolls. This is our famous Baby Head! … And so, in 1909 we came out with the new dolls and, to distinguish them from the Munich 'artist dolls', we christened them Character Dolls, a name that the whole world has since adopted."

number *114*, Hans or Gretchen, was distributed by Borgfeldt and by Strobel & Wilken (page 90).

Between 1922 and 1927, Kämmer & Reinhardt produced a doll bearing mould number *131* on a head made by Simon & Halbig, whose factory Kämmer & Reinhardt had acquired in 1920. This doll has side-glancing eyes in an impish face, with a wig, on a toddler or ball-jointed body (page 44).

Max and Moritz were two naughty boys drawn by Wilhelm Busch for a book first translated into English in 1870. Several doll making companies based dolls on these characters – indeed, some still do so to this day – among them A. Schoenhut & Co. of Philadelphia, Theodore Recknagel, Kestner, Steiff, Rheinische Gummi- und Celluloid-Fabrik and Kämmer & Reinhardt. As both characters were usually portrayed with roguish eyes and Max was given a "water melon slice" mouth, Max and Moritz may have been the forerunners of the roguish-eyed dolls. Kämmer & Reinhardt used the mould number *123* for Max and *124* for Moritz, and both were registered in 1913. The two dolls illustrated on page 100 were made by Kämmer & Reinhardt, and it is likely that the doll shown on page 101 was manufactured by Kestner.

Kämmer & Reinhardt's *Charakterpuppen* ran in a series of mould numbers from 100, which represents a six-week-old baby. This doll may have moulded hair or a wig, glass or painted eyes, be black, brown or white, and be on a bent-limb or a toddler body. Mould number *101* represents either a girl or a boy, called Marie or Peter as appropriate, and these dolls are wigged, have glass or painted eyes, closed mouths and jointed bodies (pages 78 and 81). This mould number is also found with a solid domed head with flocked hair.

Mould number *102* represents a child with a toddler body, with moulded and painted hair in a fringed style, painted eyes and a closed mouth (page 102). Mould number *103* has a wig (page 82), while mould number *104* has a moulded open/closed mouth with a "wicked" grin (page 83).

Mould numbers *105* and *106* both represent children and the dolls have wigs. Mould number *107* was called Carl; the doll has a wig and a jointed body, painted eyes and a closed mouth (pages 85 and 88).

Elise, mould number *109*, is a rather pensive-looking, almost sullen, child, with a toddler body, painted eyes and closed mouth (page 77). Mould number *112*, which could also represent either a boy or a girl, Walter or Elsa, has either a wig or flocked hair, painted or glass eyes, and a moulded open/closed mouth showing teeth. The heads are found on ball-jointed bodies (pages 76, 81 and 87).

Mould *114*, which again can represent either a boy or a girl, Hans or Gretchen, is illustrated on page 90. Mould number *115*, which was produced between 1911 and 1927, has moulded hair, a closed mouth, glass eyes and a jointed toddler body. It is interesting to note that some of Käthe Kruse's dolls resemble this particular mould number, and the two companies were connected in as much as Kämmer & Reinhardt handled Käthe Kruse's dolls. Mould number *115A*, which may be seen on page 86, was also made between 1911 and 1927, but it has a closed mouth and a wig.

Also issued between 1911 and 1927 were mould numbers *116* and *117*. Mould number *116* usually has moulded hair, an open/closed mouth with dimples and moulded teeth, glass "sleeping" eyes, and it comes on a toddler, bent-limb body or jointed body (page 80). Its *116A* wigged counterpart comes with either an open or an open/closed mouth on either a jointed toddler or a bent-limb baby body; it is usually a white child, although mulatto versions have occasionally been found. Mould number *117* is usually found on a jointed child's body with a wig, glass "sleeping" eyes and a closed mouth, although an open-mouth version of this doll was also manufactured (page 86).

One of the most prolific of the German doll manufacturers was a company founded *c.* 1805 at Waltershausen by **Johannes Daniel Kestner**. Little that is definite is known of the early history of the company, but J. D. Kestner did make papier mâché heads and lathe-turned wooden bodies, named Täuflinge. These had carved and painted bodies, but the term is now used to refer to all baby dolls produced at Waltershausen. By the mid-1800s, the company also made dolls' bodies of kid and fabric and wax over composition heads. In 1860, the company, under the direction of Johannes Daniel Kestner Junior, began to make glazed china and bisque heads in a newly acquired porcelain factory situated at Ohrdruf. Production continued there until the late 1930s. By the end of the 19th century, composition bodies were added to the range, and Kestner had taken out a number of patents for improvements and refinements to dolls' bodies.

In 1896, the Kestner mark was registered. It was a crown with streamers; later the simple initials *J.D.K.* were used. Kestner dolls were distributed by Borgfeldt and Butler Brothers, and it was for Borgfeldt that the company produced many of the bisque versions of well-known dolls – Kewpies, Bye-lo Baby and the Natural Baby, which was issued in 1912 in response to the new craze for character dolls. The company did, however, produce many other character dolls, including the so-called Gibson Girl lady dolls. As well as bisque heads, Kestner produced celluloid dolls, the heads made by Rheinische Gummi- und Celluloid-Fabrik. These heads bear the *J.D.K.* mark together with the "turtle" trademark of Rheinische Gummi.

Kestner registered many mould numbers for a great variety of dolls. The company's output included lady dolls, child and toddler dolls, and baby dolls, all with a wide range of facial expressions. The company also produced all-bisque dolls and dolls'-house sized dolls, Frozen Charlottes and character dolls, which included oriental and black dolls together with a version of Max and Moritz. Kestner dolls are illustrated on pages 92–103.

From 1895, **Kley & Hahn** operated a porcelain factory in Ohrdruf, making heads and bathing babies and then from 1902 introduced into its range various other dolls. The company also used bisque heads made by other companies, notably Kestner, Bähr & Pröschild, Schoenau & Hoffmeister and Hertel, Schwab & Co. In 1902, Kley & Hahn registered *Walküre* and in 1909 *Schneewittchen* (Snow White) for a range of dolls that included characters. The company also produced Snow Babies and the Majestic, Princess and Dollar Princess ranges. The main mark of Kley & Hahn showed *K. & H.* within a rectangular banner shape (page 69).

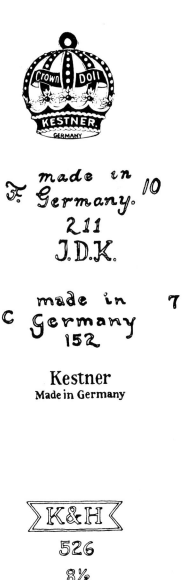

C. F. Kling & Co. was founded as a porcelain factory in 1836 at Ohrdruf by Christian Friedrich Kling. The company produced heads and complete dolls such as Frozen Charlottes, as well as jointed all-bisque dolls and Snow Babies. The trademark was a bell with the initial *K*. Like many other companies, Kling produced Bye-lo Baby heads for Borgfeldt.

König & Wernicke was established in 1912 at Waltershausen when Rudolph Wernicke replaced August and Max Rudolph in the company they had founded a year earlier with Max König. König & Wernicke produced both pretty face types and character dolls, but the company often used bisque heads made by other companies including Hertel, Schwab & Co. and celluloid heads made by the Rheinische Gummi- und Celluloid-Fabrik Co. König & Wernicke appear to have produced composition dolls' bodies and heads, although it used bisque and celluloid heads made by other companies. The company produced the bent-limb composition bodies for the Bye-lo Baby dolls for Borgfeldt. After 1945, the company continued to produce composition and other plastic dolls, gradually changing all production to vinyl.

Käthe Kruse was the wife of the sculptor, Max Kruse. She was unhappy about the dolls available for her children at the beginning of this century and decided to create her own dolls of cloth, which would appear to be more realistic. These "artistic dolls" were based on real children, and in 1910 Käthe Kruse began to make a range of dolls for other people as well as for her own family. The dolls had hand-painted muslin heads attached to stockinet bodies.

Many of Käthe Kruse's dolls were given the names of the children on whom they were modelled, although some dolls were more realistic than others. The baby dolls were especially successful, several of them designed to be the size and weight of a real baby, complete to the last detail including a coiled knob to represent a tummy button. Perhaps these baby dolls were a little too realistic to suit everyone's taste, because the toddler-type dolls proved to be much more popular. The company founded by Käthe Kruse, now situated between Nuremberg and Munich, still makes dolls that look very much like the original ones, although now they have vinyl heads. New ranges have been added, including an inexpensive range made of terry towelling. The company also runs a refurbishing scheme for older dolls.

Many Käthe Kruse designs inspired other makers to create rather realistic dolls, particularly Kämmer & Reinhardt.

The company **Gebrüder Kühnlenz** was founded in 1884 at Kronach, Bavaria, as a porcelain factory making both dolls and dolls' heads. The marks used by the company usually included the letters *Gbr* (Gebrüder) and *K.* (Kühnlenz) together with the mould numbers; sometimes the letters were encased by a round "sun" design (page 51).

Founded in 1885 at Köppelsdorf, Thüringia, the **Armand Marseille** company grew to become one of the largest manufacturers of bisque dolls' heads. The famous *A.M.* mark, coupled with the company's name, *Germany* or *Made in Germany*, and the mould number *390* is the most often seen mark, and it represented a pretty-faced socket-head, which was made for over thirty years from *c.*1900 until 1938.

Many Armand Marseille dolls' heads were produced for other companies and to specific designs. Some were for American importers such as George Borgfeldt & Co., Louis Wolf & Co., Louis Amberg & Son, Foulds & Freure, the Arranbee Doll Co. and Otto Gans. Louis Wolf & Co. of New York City was founded in 1870 as importers and handlers. The company's designs for dolls' heads were made by Armand Marseille, but it also handled many dolls from other makers both German and American. Foulds & Freure, also of New York City, was founded as importers in 1912, and Arranbee was founded ten years later in New York City as both importers and as a doll's hospital. Arranbee handled the famous My Dream Baby, which was registered by Armand Marseille in 1925 and bears the mould numbers *341* (closed mouth) and *351* (open mouth showing two teeth). Otto Gans, established at Waltershausen in 1901, was both a doll maker and an exporter of dolls. It is said that Gans invented the roguish-eye movement in 1902, and he did patent several mechanical devices for walking and talking dolls as well as for eye mechanisms.

About 1925, Armand Marseille used the word *Ellar* with the mould number *355* for an oriental-type bisque head, which was usually placed on a bent-limb body. The mould numbers around *355* (*353* and *356*) also represent oriental-type dolls (page 105).

Fany was another tradename used by Armand Marseille to represent a rather chubby child. The heads were issued with either moulded hair (mould number *230*) or with wigs (mould number *231*) (pages 102 and 106). Mould number *550* shows a slightly smiling character face with a closed mouth, "sleeping" eyes and a wig (page 121), while mould number *252* (page 47), which was sold by Borgfeldt, represents a googly-type doll with roguish eyes, a "water melon slice" smiling mouth and moulded hair.

The doll shown on page 107, bearing the mould number *700*, was most probably made by Armand Marseille. It is worth noting, however, that this mould number was used also by Kämmer & Reinhardt for a baby doll similar to the company's first 1909 doll, which bears the mould number *100*. Usually, however, the Kämmer & Reinhardt mould number *700* doll appears with a celluloid head, made by the Rheinische Gummi- und Celluloid-Fabrik Company. In the late 1920s the number *700* was also used by the Italian firm Lenci for its felt dolls Dina, Rita and Edvidge. Lenci was the tradename of a Turin-based company, which was founded in 1920 and continues to make dolls today, including some re-issues of original 1920s and 1930s designs. Like the dolls made by Käthe Kruse, Lenci dolls were individually modelled on real children, and although many of the dolls have rather sullen expressions, they have great charm and are much sought after by collectors today.

Armand Marseille created all sorts of dolls, many of them character dolls, but many were straightforward pretty dolls with happy facial expressions. These proved to be the most popular in the long term, and hundreds of thousands of such dolls were made. Marseille also developed new techniques and styles as well as taking advantage of advances made by other manufacturers as they appeared – "sleeping" eyes, roguish eyes, intaglio eyes; dolls representing different races or nations; and dolls with different

Made in Germany
Armand Marseille
560a
A ⁴⁄₀ M
D.R.M.R. 232

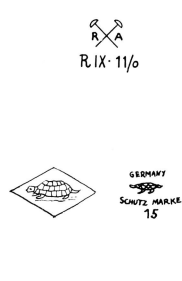

body types and made of a variety of materials: composition, jointed kid, and celluloid, combined with the occasional use of rubber, particularly for hands (pages 105–9).

Theodor Recknagel founded a hard-paste porcelain factory at Alexandrienthal near Oeslau, Thüringia, in 1886. Using the initials *R.* and *A.* with the mould numbers, the company registered many designs, and it may have made the left-hand doll shown on page 49 (attributed to Gebrüder Kühnlenz) as mould number 55 was one for a character doll registered by the company in 1914. However, as with many other mould numbers, 55 was registered by other companies too. The right-hand doll on page 116 was one of the company's black dolls, which they had begun to manufacture in 1897 with the issue of both a black and a mulatto (light brown) head.

The **Rheinische Gummi- und Celluloid-Fabrik Co.** was established in 1873 initially to make rubber products but adding celluloid items in 1880. The company still produces dolls today under the name of *Schildkröt*, the German word for turtle, the company's trademark. Rheinische Gummi made both rubber and celluloid dolls, often on behalf of other companies and to their specific design. The turtle trademark, which was registered in 1899, is said to represent the durability and long life of the company's products.

Throughout its history, the company produced dolls for other companies, sometimes working with a straightforward copy of a bisque mould and at other times making a new design for a head.

When Rheinische Gummi made a head or whole doll on behalf of another company, both manufacturers' trademarks appeared on the head. Many dolls with bisque or composition heads had body parts made of celluloid, and these parts bear the turtle trademark alone.

Bruno Schmidt was established in 1900 at Waltershausen, and the company produced bisque, composition and celluloid dolls in various designs, including baby, oriental and character dolls. In 1918 the company acquired the porcelain factory at Ohrdruf of Bähr & Pröschild. Bruno Schmidt's main trademarks were often based on a heart shape (page 39).

Franz Schmidt & Co. was established in 1890 at Georgenthal near Waltershausen. The steam-operated factory produced dolls of different materials – bisque, wood, composition and cellulobrim (a form of celluloid) – in many different designs. Occasionally the company used heads made by other manufacturers, including Simon & Halbig. Franz Schmidt applied for various patents, covering improvements to eyes, facial features such as noses and teeth, and walking mechanisms. The chief trademarks used included the initials *F.S. & C.* and *S. & C.,* together with the marks of any other maker involved, such as Simon & Halbig. Alt, Beck & Gottschalck was the other primary producer of bisque heads for Franz Schmidt & Co., the most commonly found of these being mould number *1272*, a character baby with an open mouth, two teeth, open nostrils and, usually, a solid-domed head (page 38).

Simon & Halbig was established at Ohrdruf at Gräfenhain in 1869 as a porcelain factory making many other products as well as dolls' heads. The company developed rapidly, and the heads it made are plentiful, surpassed in numbers found today only by those produced by Armand Marseille. In addition to manufacturing dolls' heads for Kämmer & Reinhardt, Simon & Halbig made heads for many other companies, both French and German, including Heinrich Handwerck, Charles M. Bergmann, Cuno & Otto Dressel, Franz Schmidt and Hamburger & Co. Simon & Halbig heads have even been found on marked Jumeau bodies, and many S.F.B.J. dolls had heads supplied by the German company.

Simon & Halbig dolls' heads are usually marked with mould numbers, and each number was used only by one company. Thus it would appear that Simon & Halbig produced specific heads under the direction of one company, rather than supplying heads to allcomers indiscriminately. Occasionally, if more than one company was involved in the production of a doll, it is probable that each company assembled, designed or made the various parts of the individual doll.

Simon & Halbig worked closely with Kämmer & Reinhardt in the production of the character dolls numbered within the 100 range. The company became part of Kämmer & Reinhardt in 1920 and thus part of the larger Bing Werke, which Kämmer & Reinhardt had joined two years earlier. Bing Werke was founded by Gebrüder Bing, the toy making company best known for the manufacture of toy cars, trains and various tin and mechanical items.

The quality of the bisque used by Simon & Halbig was very good, and the company's expertise in modelling, painting and design were extremely high. Many styles were produced – baby, child and lady dolls were most common – while it also created character dolls and early figures with elaborate moulded hairstyles, often decorated with flowers, hats and snoods all moulded as one and delicately painted and enhanced with lustre colours. The company also used many variations of facial design – glass eyes, both "sleeping" and static; pierced ears and nostrils; and closed, open and open/closed mouths with or without teeth. Similar heads have been found that have all possible variations or just some of them.

Simon & Halbig trademarks vary; early dolls usually have only the initials *S.H.* (page 121), revised to *S. & H.* in 1905 (page 122); others have the whole name written in full. Usually mould numbers are included; occasionally they are Roman numerals like the example shown on page 121. Mould number *1308* (page 78), although a character face, came in three known versions – possibly more – representing a coke burner, a man with a moustache and a girl in regional costume.

Mould number *150* (pages 84, 89 and 117), while not marked for Kämmer & Reinhardt, was a painted-eyed character face produced for that company. The lady doll, mould number *1303* (page 85), was also produced as a child with painted or glass eyes. (The words *Wimpern Geschütz* refer to the eyelashes.) Mould numbers *1388* (page 118), *1398* (page 123), *153* (page 122) and *1279* (page 115) were all character faces, and the latter was known to have been used by Charles M. Bergmann.

Simon & Halbig made black and mulatto (light brown) dolls as well as white and oriental dolls. Some of these dolls were from the same moulds, but of differently coloured bisque, while others were more physically

SH 1080 DEP 7

1358
Germany
SIMON & HALBIG
S&H
5

correct for the race intended. Such was the case with mould numbers *1358* and *1368* (page 116).

Among the character dolls made by Simon & Halbig were some fine lady dolls with specially designed bodies. Two such dolls, mould numbers *152* and *1305*, are illustrated on pages 119 and 120 respectively.

Margarete Steiff founded a company in 1877 at Giengen, Württemberg. The mainstay of this German company was soft toy animals made of velvet, plush and felt. Although at first Margarete Steiff also made dolls' clothes, dolls themselves were not added to the range until 1889, when dolls with mask heads were introduced. In 1894, nine styles of dolls with unbreakable heads, felt bodies and clothes were advertised, together with dolls with porcelain heads. The two main characteristics of Steiff dolls are the central seam down the face and the "button in the ear" (*Knopf im Ohr*), a small metal disc attached through the left ear of each doll or toy.

Each Steiff doll was made to an individual design, usually representing a person or occupation or wearing national or regional costume. Many were also comic, based on clowns or on characters of the day, including some from children's literature. Steiff dolls and toys were very popular and were exported all over the world. They are extremely desirable and greatly sought after today.

Swaine & Co. was established in 1854 at Hüttensteinach near Sonneberg and continued as a hard-paste porcelain factory until 1918, when it joined with Gebrüder Schoenau. After 1927 the production of dolls ceased. Although not yet fully proven, it is thought that the green circular stamp with the initials *S. & C.* found on dolls with bisque heads, represents this company (page 112).

The French Connection

During the last thirty years of the 19th century, the leading French doll manufacturers produced some very beautiful character-type dolls as well as some horrors. The companies often employed artists and sculptors to design the heads, and they used delicate painting methods to create what may well be termed as works of art. The skin tone of French dolls was more natural, especially when compared with the stark reds and whites used by the German makers at the same time. In the 1860s and 1870s, German makers were only beginning to introduce pink-toned glazes. Blown glass eyes of different shades of blue and brown were another important feature of the early French dolls.

Throughout the 1860s and 1870s, the majority of French dolls were fashion-type dolls with stuffed kid bodies, shaped to resemble the figure of an adult woman. The dolls were dressed in the latest Parisian styles, and the clothes were often made by dressmakers using remnants of materials used to make the full-sized costumes. Gradually, the design of the dolls shifted from the fashion model to the more natural looking child doll, although even then many of the dolls were still fashionably dressed. The French doll industry was centred in Paris, later moving to the outskirts of the city and to other places such as Limoges.

There were three main manufacturers – Steiner, Jumeau and Bru. It may be that these companies made as well as designed their dolls, but it is now thought that they also imported heads from Germany or employed German makers to make dolls to their own specifications. It is not possible in all cases to state categorically which was actually the case, and, unless otherwise known, the dolls and their manufacture are attributed to the company whose marks are shown on the heads or bodies. After all, that company instigated the doll, whether it made it or not.

The initials *E.B.* are now attributed to the Parisian doll makers **E. Barrois** and **Mme Aimable Ange Lucienne Barrois**, who were among the earliest French makers to use glazed china and bisque dolls' heads. Recorded as being in business from 1844 until 1877, E. Barrois produced standard dolls, poupards and mechanical dolls of a variety of materials, importing heads of different types from Germany, including composition and porcelain ones. Among the mechanical dolls found bearing the *E.B.* mark are *Autoperipatetikos* dolls.

The makers produced both shoulder-head and swivel-head dolls. The eyes could be painted or of glass. Generally, the dolls are found with wigs of human or animal hair, and their ears are pierced. The mouths are closed and delicately painted, with high "bows" on the top lip and a deep central lower lip, giving a look of a rather pursed mouth (page 40).

One of *the* great French doll making companies was founded by Casimer (Casimir) Bru in 1866. Casimer remained with the company, known as **Bru Jne. & Cie.,** until 1883, after which it changed directors a number of times before amalgamating with other French firms to form the Société Française de Fabrication de Bébés et Jouets (S.F.B.J.) in 1899.

Bru dolls were luxury products, although not as expensive as those by Jumeau, and they have fine bisque heads and bodies of wood, kid and composition. There is some question now whether Bru actually made the heads or had them made by other companies. Casimer Bru himself introduced many inventions, especially for mechanical devices, and he may have been an innovator rather than a maker. He designed crying and feeding dolls, two-faced dolls and dolls with special eye movements. He also designed different body types – extensively jointed wooden ones, gusseted and jointed kid ones and bodies of composition with kid. The company's early dolls had bisque shoulder-heads or swivel-heads mounted on gusseted kid bodies, fashioned to an adult shape. Later, while retaining parts of the gusseted kid body and the swivel-heads, the hands were also moulded from bisque. This change was incorporated when the *Bébé Bru* doll line was introduced in 1872. In addition to making lady and child dolls, although not baby dolls, the company produced life-sized heads for shop manikins.

Many of Bru's early lady dolls have smiling faces. Rather than just imparting a pleasing expression, the mouths are tilted upward dramatically. Glass eyes were used, surrounded by long and quite dense painted lashes on both upper and lower lids. The *Bébé Bru* dolls, which were made in greater numbers after 1880, often have moulded open mouths showing teeth and a tongue; these are not necessarily the most attractive dolls of their day but are much sought after today.

BRU J^{ne} R
BREVETE S.G.D.G.
Y 8 M

BRU. J^{ne} R
11

Among Bru's mechanical innovations were two-faced dolls showing a happy face and a sleeping, crying or sad face. After 1870, several doll makers produced multi-faced dolls, some with up to four faces, which were generally revealed by turning the head around on a spindle. The dolls shown on pages 41–3 may all have been made by Bru, but, as they are unmarked cannot be proven; on the other hand, the company may have used heads made by another manufacturer.

In common with many other companies of the time, Bru designed dolls of different colours to represent different races. The oriental doll shown on page 6 is one such example. It bears one of the standard marks, *Bru Jne.*, and the head colour has been matched by staining the kid body. In this case the head and lower arms are of bisque and the lower legs of wood. The company used a variety of different hair materials for the wigs, including fleece. Such wigs, of lambswool or other animal fur, retained the skin backing, which was stretched and glued over the head. Bru also used the more conventional mohair-on-canvas wig types.

After 1899, when Bru became part of the S.F.B.J., its doll *Bébé Bru* continued to be made until the 1950s. Other inventions, such as the Kiss Throwing mechanism, have been found on S.F.B.J marked dolls. During the 1880s and 1890s, Bru was awarded a number of medals and honourable mentions in various international expositions.

Another early French doll making concern was the **Maison Huret**, which was said to have been founded as early as 1812 and was still in business in the 1930s. The quality of the dolls produced by the company varied tremendously from highly sought after bisque lady fashion dolls to cheap souvenir types sold at the seaside. Many of the dolls represented national characters and pierrots. The company produced dolls with heads of all materials – glazed china, bisque, wood, composition and metal, with either glass or painted eyes. Huret dolls are often found with jointed wooden bodies, and they sometimes have metal hands. Many of the Huret dolls, like those of Bru, had fleece wigs, but these were gradually replaced by the more easily fashioned mohair wigs (pages 58–63).

The **Jumeau** family of doll makers was established by Pierre Jumeau in Paris in 1842, and dolls continued to be made until the company became part of the S.F.B.J. in 1899. With a factory complex at Montreuil-sous-Bois, the company made not only the dolls' wood and kid bodies, but also the clothing, adding kilns in 1873 to fire the heads as well.

At first, Jumeau used shaped kid bodies and jointed wooden ones. Composition bodies were added in the 1870s when Jumeau began to make *bébé*-type dolls. (This was the term applied to a doll representing a child from babyhood to the age of about six years, and many of the dolls called *bébé* were, in fact, of the older group rather than of babies.)

As well as straightforward lady dolls and child dolls, the company manufactured character dolls, possibly modelled on real children by known artists and sculptors, dolls representing different races – white, black and mulatto – and two-faced dolls. The company also made a few mechanical dolls, including walking and talking examples. Throughout its history, the Jumeau company received much acclaim, and during the 1880s and 1890s it

won many international awards for its dolls and their bodies and their clothes (pages 2 and 64–75).

Jumeau used dolls' heads that had been made by other companies, including German ones. Simon & Halbig heads have been found on Jumeau dolls, and after 1899, the S.F.B.J. issued Jumeau dolls, continuing to re-issue them until the 1950s.

In 1899, a group of French doll makers gathered together to form an association to assist the makers in their competition with the ever-increasing German imports. By the end of the 19th century the German products were cheaper and often better in quality than the French, and it became a grave worry to the French makers. About ten companies amalgamated to form the **Société Française de Fabrication de Bébés et Jouets**, ironically under the leadership of Saloman Fleischmann of Fleischmann & Bloedel of Fürth, Sonneberg and Paris. Each company donated the rights to one of its dolls, usually a *bébé*, and those companies that had porcelain factories leased them for the making of the heads.

Using the existing dolls and introducing other inventions and innovations, the S.F.B.J. produced many hundreds of dolls, adopting the initials S.F.B.J. as its trademark in 1905. In many cases, the quality of its dolls gradually deteriorated (as they did in Germany, too). The S.F.B.J. reissued various dolls a number of times, right up to the 1950s; these included the *Bébé Bru*, the *Bébé Jumeau* and the *Eden Bébé* (pages 125–9).

Jules Nicholas Steiner was the maker of some very rare and special dolls. Established in 1855, the company continued to make dolls until 1908; they were of every kind including lady and *bébé* dolls. However, it is in the field of mechanical dolls that Steiner shone, particularly the combined walking and talking dolls, which were also elegantly dressed. Many early Steiner dolls have a double row of teeth, cast in with the moulded head. These are not always pleasant to look at, as the doll's smile can sometimes resemble a grimace. In addition to these dolls, Steiner produced coloured dolls representing different races and a few representing different occupations, including a clown or a pierrot (pages 130–1).

Incised on the head of Baby Bo-Kaye is the mark *1307–124 Germany*, and it is possible that the doll's head was manufactured by Alt, Beck & Gottschalck of Nauendorf, Germany. The hair is moulded, the brown glass eyes are fixed, and the mouth is open. The doll is 17in (43cm) tall. The body is cloth, although the lower arms and legs are composition.

In the box is an all-bisque Baby Bo-Kaye. It has joints at the neck, shoulders and hips and is 5in (13cm) tall. American designer Joseph L. Kallus designed the Baby Bo-Kaye dolls, which were distributed by George Borgfeldt & Co. *c*.1926.

The bald-headed toddler, which was made by the German firm Alt, Beck & Gottschalck, bears the incised mark *A.B.G. 4/0 1322/23*. It is 10in (25cm) tall. The blue glass eyes are fixed, and two teeth may be seen in the open mouth. The jointed body, which has side hip joints, is made of composition.

Grace Storey Putnam's Fly-lo Baby is one of the rarest bisque-head dolls ever produced. The doll illustrated here is 12in (30cm) tall, and its bisque head bears the incised mark *Copyright by Grace S. Putnam Made in Germany*; it was probably manufactured by Alt, Beck & Gottschalck. The body is cloth, and the hands are celluloid. The blue "sleeping" eyes are of glass, the mouth is closed, and the hair is deeply sculpted. Fly-lo Baby was made also with a composition head. It is believed that the doll was produced as a "Lindbergh baby" but was withdrawn from manufacture when the child was kidnapped.

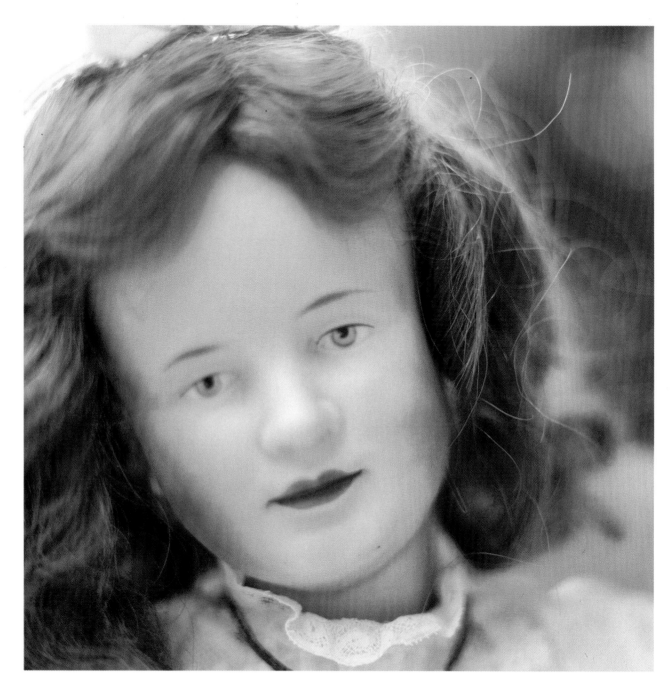

This doll's head bears the incised mark *Deponirt F.S. & Co. 1262/50* for Franz Schmidt & Co., the doll manufacturers from Georgenthal, Thüringia. The company used heads made by a number of manufacturers, and it is possible that the head seen here was produced by Alt, Beck & Gottschalck. The blue eyes are painted, and the mouth is closed. The jointed body is composition, and the doll is 20½ in (52cm) tall.

It is thought that the heads of both these dolls were made for Bruno Schmidt of Waltershausen by Bähr & Pröschild of Thüringia. The smaller doll, which is 13½in (34cm) tall, bears the incised number *2069 149 1*. The blue glass eyes move, and the mouth is closed; the doll's jointed body is of composition.

The doll on the right, often referred to as Wendy although that was not the doll's factory name, is 17½in (45cm) tall. Incised on the back of the head is the mark *2033 B.S.W.* [in a heart] *537*. The blue glass eyes move, the mouth is closed, and the jointed body is of composition.

This doll, which bears the incised mark *E.B. Déposé*, is attributed to E. Barrois, the Paris-based manufacturer and distributor of porcelain and paste dolls' heads. The fixed eyes are of brown glass, and the open/closed mouth reveals teeth. The doll is 18in (46cm) tall and has a jointed wood and composition body. The outfit is original to the doll.

RIGHT
This extremely rare French doll is attributed to the Parisian firm of Bru. As early as 1867 the firm had patented a two-faced doll, and the doll illustrated here, with one laughing face and one crying face, was made *c.*1880. The flange neck is decorated with a moulded necklace, and a wooden rod, running inside the head down into the shoulder-plate, helps the head to rotate to reveal the two faces. The bisque head is mounted on a kid body, and the doll is 14in (36cm) tall.

In the pram, which was manufactured *c.*1910 by the German company Märklin and is of enamelled and painted tin, is a French bisque-head doll with a five-piece bisque body, swivel head and glass eyes. The doll was manufactured *c.*1890 and is wearing its original clothes and mohair wig.

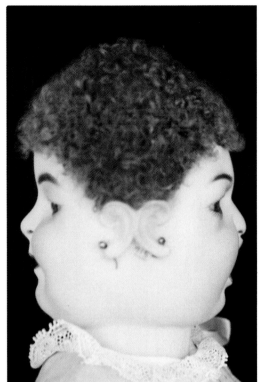

Although this doll is unmarked, it is attributed to Bru, which had patented a similar doll. The fixed eyes are blue glass, and the ears are applied. On one face the mouth is closed; on the other, the "screamer", the mouth is open/closed. The French-style jointed body is of wood. Both faces of this doll may be found, separately, on automata. The doll is 18in (46cm) tall.

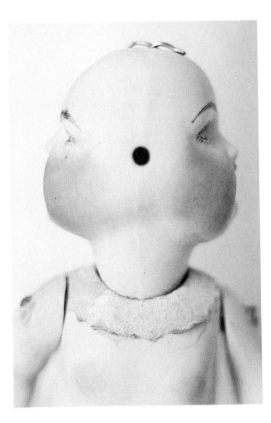

This unmarked, two-faced doll is attributed to Bru, the only manufacturer to include breasts on its moulded bodies. The blue eyes are painted, and the mouth on the "screamer" face is open/closed and shows moulded teeth. The doll is 9in (23cm) tall. The five-piece body is all bisque, a swivel neck allowing the head to move to reveal the two faces. The shoes and socks are moulded.

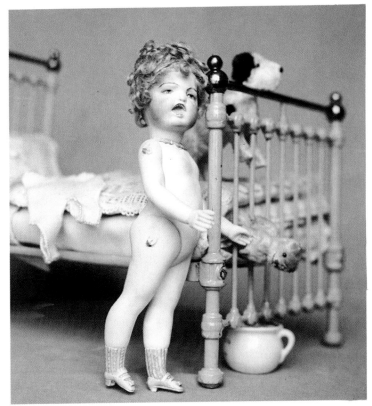

All the dolls illustrated here are generally referred to by collectors as googlies – dolls with roguish or side-glancing eyes. The left-hand doll is incised *J.D.K. 221 Geschütz* and was manufactured by J.D. Kestner of Waltershausen, Thüringia. The blue "sleeping" eyes glance to the side, and the good quality toddler body, with unjointed wrists, is of composition. The doll is 13in (33cm) tall. Although not particularly rare, the doll is one of the most popular of all the googlies among collectors.

Second from left is a doll with the incised mark *173*. Once thought to have been manufactured by J.D. Kestner, it is now believed that the doll was made by the German porcelain company Hertel, Schwab & Co. The "sleeping" eyes are side-glancing, and the lips of the closed mouth are slightly pursed. The doll is 16in (41cm) tall, and the body is, in typical toddler style, fully jointed, including wrist and side hip joints. The clothes and blond wig of human hair are original to the doll.

The doll in the centre of the group bears a strong resemblance to the Campbell Kid dolls, a series of American dolls in a variety of dresses advertising soups (see page 133). The doll is 13½in (34cm) tall and bears the incised mark *163*. It was manufactured by Hertel, Schwab & Co. The blue "sleeping" eyes glance to the side, and the mouth is the so-called "water melon" mouth; the carrot-coloured hair is moulded as are the orange shoes and white socks. The toddler-style body is unusual in being fully jointed except at the knees, and the legs are straight.

The doll second from right bears the incised mark *K. [star] R. Simon & Halbig 131*. The large, round blue glass eyes "sleep" and are sideways glancing; the eyebrows are sharply arched. Another version of this doll has the more usual "half-moon" shaped eyebrows painted above the glass eyes. The doll, which is 15½in (39cm) tall, has a fully jointed composition body.

The right-hand doll has a composition mask-face over a cloth head with a mohair wig. The eyes are glass. It is thought that the doll was manufactured by the German company Eisenmann & Co., Fürth. Eisenmann took out a patent in 1905 for moulded cardboard faces for its rag dolls. The cardboard was covered with a layer of coloured gauze, which was then painted, and eye sockets were cut in the cardboard for inset eyes. The type of doll seen here is found also with a bisque head on a jointed composition body; such dolls were produced by Gebrüder Heubach of Lichte, Thüringia.

Bearing only the incised mark *134 5*,
the doll was possibly manufactured by
Hertel, Schwab & Co. The blue glass
eyes move and the mouth is closed.
The doll, which is $16\frac{1}{2}$in (42cm) tall,
has a jointed composition body.

Both dolls illustrated here were manufactured by Gebrüder Heubach of Lichte, Thüringia, Germany. The girl doll bears the incised number *7764* and the sunburst mark of Gebrüder Heubach. It is 13¾in (35cm) tall and has an open/closed mouth and intaglio eyes glancing to the side. The deeply moulded hair is topped by a moulded pink bow. The five-piece baby body with bent limbs is marked *F.A.O. Schwartz, New York.*

The boy doll is also incised with Gebrüder Heubach's sunburst mark and with the number *7622*. The doll is 20½in (52cm) tall. The intaglio eyes are blue, and the mouth is closed. The moulded face has deep dimples, and there are three tufts of curly, moulded hair, one in the centre of the forehead and one above each ear. The jointed composition body is of good quality, and the doll's outfit dates from *c.*1910.

All the googly-eyed dolls illustrated here have painted eyes and bisque heads. The left-hand doll was manufactured by Gebrüder Heubach. It is 5in (13cm) tall and is wearing its original cloth shift and leather shoes.

The Steiff character animal – which is known as "Billy Possum" – was manufactured c.1905. It is 11in (28cm) tall and has fully jointed arms, legs, head and tail.

In front of "Billy Possum" is another all-bisque doll by Gebrüder Heubach. It too is 5in (13cm) tall and is wearing its original shift and leather shoes.

At the front of the group is a Campbell Kid (see page 133). Also 5in (13cm) tall, it has a four-piece, jointed bisque body and a non-swivel neck.

The right-hand doll was manufactured by Armand Marseille. It is incised with the number *252* and has a moulded top-knot, intaglio, side-glancing eyes and a smiling mouth. The five-piece baby body is of composition, and the doll is 9½in (24cm) tall. It was marketed in New York c.1915 by George Borgfeldt & Co.

This Gebrüder Heubach toddler is incised with the mould number *81 45*; it also bears the Heubach square mark and the word *Germany*. Its side-glancing eyes are painted on the bisque head. The composition toddler-style body has side hip joints. The *art deco* boy's dress is contemporary with the doll.

The doll on the left bears the incised number *55-37*, and it is possible that it was manufactured by the German company Gebrüder Kühnlenz, which is known to have incised hyphenated numbers on the back of the dolls' heads it produced. The doll is 23½in (60cm) tall and has an open mouth with four square, moulded teeth coming from the upper lip and a slight opening between the teeth and the lower lip. The grey-blue eyes are fixed, and the wood and composition body is similar to those found on early Simon & Halbig dolls, with a large amount of wood in the upper legs. The doll is probably earlier than many of those illustrated in this book.

The right-hand doll bears the mould number *83 16* of Gebrüder Heubach. The doll is extremely rare and has the square Heubach mark and the size number *7* incised on the back of the head. The eyes are of glass, the head is open crown with a wig, and the open/closed mouth has eight, tiny moulded teeth.

Illustrated here, surrounded by Steiff animals, are character dolls by, left, Gebrüder Heubach and, right, Armand Marseille. The Gebrüder Heubach doll is a mould number *2850* doll. The jointed composition body is of only average quality, and the doll is 15in (39cm) tall. The open/closed mouth has two rows of moulded teeth with the tongue protruding between them. The eyes are intaglio, and the moulded hair has braids pulled around the back of the head with a blue moulded ribbon forming a bow in the centre. The peasant costume is contemporary with the doll.

The right-hand doll is incised *A. 5 M.* It has an open/closed mouth and six moulded teeth. The intaglio eyes are deep set, and the mohair wig is original to the doll. The jointed composition body is of moderately good quality, and the doll is 15¾in (40cm) tall. The original costume probably represents the Ukraine region of Russia.

The left-hand doll of these three fired-in-bisque black character dolls was manufactured by Gebrüder Heubach. It bears the mould number *76 68*, the Heubach sunburst mark, the word *Germany* and the incised number *2*, which indicates head size. The doll, which is 10¼in (26cm) tall, has a five-piece baby body with bent limbs. The deep intaglio brown eyes are sideways glancing, and the open/closed mouth has red, fired-in-bisque lips. It is wearing its original shift.

The doll in the centre is incised with the number *34-29*. The open mouth has four moulded teeth, and the jointed composition body is in the French style. It used to be thought that the doll was manufactured by the S.F.B.J., but it is now believed that the head was made in Germany for export to France either by Gebrüder Heubach or by Gebrüder Kühnlenz. Unusually, the black colour is fired on both sides of the bisque – that is, the inside as well as the outside of the head is coloured black. On the majority of black bisque heads the colour is fired only over the outside of the head while the inside is left white.

The right-hand doll is a Gebrüder Heubach mould number *76 61*. It bears the incised Heubach sunburst mark, the word *Germany* and the number *1*, which indicates size. The five-piece baby body has bent limbs. The open/closed mouth has widely parted lips, and the intaglio eyes glance sideways to the right. There are deeply moulded tufts of hair on the top of the doll's head and forehead. The doll is 9in (23cm) tall and is wearing its original orange and white striped and polka dot patterned romper suit.

Illustrated here is one of a series of character girl dolls manufactured by Gebrüder Heubach between 1910 and 1920. The doll bears the incised mark *83 81 Heubach* [in a square] *Germany*. The blue eyes are painted and the mouth is closed. The hair and hair ribbon are moulded, and the dolls in the series are distinguished by the different style of ribbons in their hair. The joined body is of composition, and the doll is 17in (43cm) tall.

The small doll is all bisque and has joints at shoulders and hips and a swivel waist. The eyes are painted, and the doll bears the incised mark *270–15 Germany*.

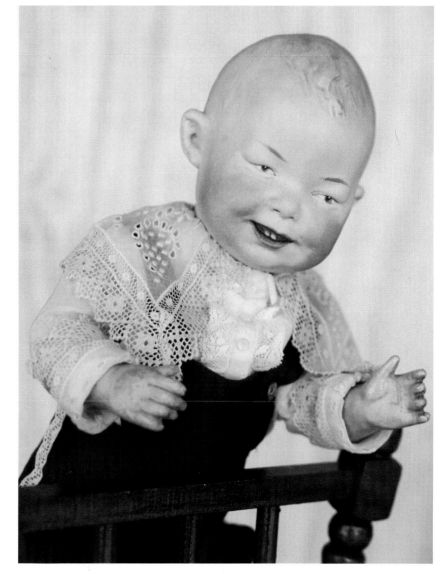

The Gebrüder Heubach toddler bears the incised number *77 45* and the Heubach sunburst mark. The blue eyes are painted, and the open/closed mouth has two moulded lower teeth. The doll is 15in (38cm) tall, and the fully jointed toddler body has fixed wrists. The hair is moulded.

Made between 1910 and 1920, this
baby doll with moulded hair bears the
incised mould number *85 56 Heubach*
[in a square] *Germany.* The mouth is
open/closed, and the intaglio eyes are
blue. The doll is 15in (38cm) tall, and
its five-piece composition body has
bent limbs.

This Gebrüder Heubach doll bears the incised mark *4 Heubach* [in a square] *Germany*. The blue glass eyes are fixed, and in the open/closed mouth five small moulded teeth and the tip of the moulded tongue are visible. The doll is wearing its original blond mohair wig. Its jointed composition body has fixed wrists and the doll is 13in (33cm) tall.

This small googly-eyed doll – it is 12½in (32cm) tall – was manufactured by Gebrüder Heubach and bears the incised mark *3 Heubach* [in a square] *85 90*. The blue eyes are painted, the hair is moulded, and the closed mouth is faintly smiling. The composition body is fully jointed, including the wrists.

The shoulder-head doll with the moulded braids of hair – ram's horns – above its ears, bears the incised mark *3 Heubach* [in a square] *Germany 78 52*. The painted blue eyes glance to the doll's right, and five moulded upper teeth are visible in the open/closed mouth. The doll, which stands 15in (38cm) tall, has a pink cloth body and bisque lower arms and hands.

Although this "crying" doll bears only the incised mark *0120 18*, it is attributed to Heubach. The mouth is open/closed, and the blue eyes are painted. The doll, which has a German-style, jointed composition body, is 28in (71cm) tall.

Pictured next to its original box is a "Tinie Baby". Although the box bears a label with the words "E.I. Horsman Co. Inc., New York", the doll itself is incised with the words *1924 by E.I. Horsman Co Inc Germany 43*. The doll is 9in (23cm) tall. Its blue glass eyes move, and its mouth is closed. The five-piece baby body, which has bent limbs, is all bisque. The doll's head has an open crown, covered by a wig, which is rarer than the closed-crown version of the same doll.

Both of these Huret character dolls have closed mouths and glass eyes, and both are 19in (48cm) tall. The girl doll has the bulbous neck that is typical of Huret dolls; the jointed body is wooden and the hands are pewter. The outfit resembles a walking-out dress of the 1880s, and the blond mohair wig is topped by a green and lavender silk hat decorated with cloth flowers. The man doll bears the incised mark *Huret* on the back of the head and also on the jointed wooden body. The doll's hands are pewter, but, unlike its companion, it has a swivel joint at the waist. The very white bisque of its head contrasts sharply with its red lips. The doll is dressed to represent Punchinello.

SEE PREVIOUS PAGES

Not only is this doll incised on the back of the neck with the name *Huret*, it also bears the incised words *Huret, 50 rue de la Boette* on the back of its wooden body. The doll's blue eyes are painted and its mouth is closed. The doll, which is 18in (46cm) tall, has a swivel joint at the neck, but the other joints are tenon joints.

Although unmarked, the doll seated in the chair has a jointed wooden body that is typical of Huret dolls. The blue eyes are painted, and the mouth is closed. The doll is 17in (43cm) tall. The small all-bisque doll was manufactured by William Goebel.

The head of this "whistling" boy doll bears the words *Déposé Jumeau* printed in red and the incised number *205*. The blue glass eyes are fixed, the mouth is open, and the ears are applied. The doll is actually an automaton, of which both the head and arms move when the mechanism is operated. The doll itself is 21in (53cm) tall, but the overall height of the automaton, including the box on which it stands, is 26in (66cm).

RIGHT
The words *Déposé Jumeau 11* are printed and the number *201* is incised on this doll's head. The mouth is open/closed, the brown glass eyes are fixed, and the ears are applied. The doll, which is 24in (61cm) tall, has a jointed wood and composition body with wrist joints.

This "screaming" doll has printed in red on its head the mark *Déposé Tête Jumeau* √ √ *M4*; incised on the head is the number *11*. The blue glass eyes are fixed, the mouth is open/closed, and the ears are applied. The wood and composition Jumeau body has wrist joints, and the doll is 22in (56cm) tall. This type of head, in a smaller size, may be found on automata.

Although the head bears only the incised number *214*, the doll's body bears a Jumeau mark printed in blue. As with other similar Jumeau dolls, the blue glass eyes are fixed, the mouth is open/closed, and the ears are applied. The doll, which is 23in (59cm) tall, has a wood and composition body with fixed wrists.

This Jumeau doll bears the mark *223 Déposé Jumeau Bte. S.G.D.G. 11*. The mould number *(223)* and size *(11)* are incised; the other words are printed in red. The doll is 22in (56cm) tall and has fixed brown glass eyes and a closed mouth. The ears are applied. The jointed body is composition, and the limbs are wooden. The letters *S.G.D.G.*, which are found only on French dolls, stand for *Sans Garantie du Gouvernement* and indicate that a patent or trademark has not yet been guaranteed by the French government. The series of character dolls produced by Jumeau begins with mould number *201* and ends with number *225*; the S.F.B.J. character series follows on from mould number *226*.

In the bootee-shaped cot are two Bye-lo baby dolls. Marked *Copyright Grace S. Putnam*, the dolls have bisque heads with painted features, cloth bodies and composition hands.

The "laughing" Jumeau bears the
mark *Déposé Tête Jumeau Bte. S.G.D.G.
12*. The glass eyes are fixed, the mouth
is open/closed and the ears are applied.
The doll is 26in (66cm) tall.

Printed in red on the head of the
"crying" Jumeau doll is the mark
Déposé Tête Jumeau Bte. S.G.D.G.; the
head is also marked with the incised
figure *10*. The doll is 22in (56cm) tall.
The brown glass eyes are fixed, the
mouth is closed, and the ears are
applied. The Jumeau-style body is of
jointed wood and composition, but the
wrists are fixed.

This "worried" Jumeau doll is 28in (71cm) tall, and it bears the mark *Déposé Tête Jumeau* printed in red on its head. The blue glass eyes are fixed, the mouth is open/closed, and the ears are applied. The jointed wood and composition body is typical of Jumeau.

The baby doll, which has brown glass eyes, has moulded hair. It bears the incised mark *126–0 Germany*, and its five-piece composition body has bent limbs. It is 9in (23cm) tall.

The "smiling" Jumeau boy doll, wearing a Mardi Gras costume, has a red armband with the words *Bébé Jumeau* on it. The doll's head bears the mark *Déposé Tête Jumeau* printed in red and the incised mould number *203* and size *11*. The doll's brown glass eyes are fixed, and its mouth is open/closed; the ears are applied. The Jumeau-type jointed body, which has movable wrists, is of composition and wood, and the doll is 25 in (64cm) tall. This doll is illustrated also on page 2.

The Jumeau girl doll, wearing a French regional costume, bears the printed mark *Déposé Tête Jumeau Bte. S.G.D.G.* and the incised mark *225 12*. The blue glass eyes are fixed, the mouth is closed, and the ears are applied. The doll is 26 in (66cm) tall, and its Jumeau-type jointed wood and composition body has fixed wrists.

The head of this Jumeau "screamer" bears the words *Déposé Tête Jumeau* printed in red and the incised numbers *211 10*. The fixed eyes are of brown glass, the mouth is open/closed, and the ears are applied. The doll is 23in (59cm) tall, and it has a jointed Jumeau-type body of wood and composition with fixed wrists.

RIGHT

This coffee-coloured doll is attributed to Jumeau, the only mark on the head being the incised number *218*, which is one of the mould numbers used by the company. The brown glass eyes are fixed, the mouth is open/closed, and the ears are applied. The wood and composition Jumeau-type body has jointed wrists. The doll stands 25in (64cm) tall.

This Kämmer & Reinhardt doll bears the incised mark K. [star] R. *112*; incised at the base of the neck is the figure *54* to indicate height in centimetres – i.e., 21¼in. The blue eyes are painted, and the doll's mouth is open/closed with two moulded upper teeth and a moulded tongue protruding below the teeth and just above the lower lip. The doll's rather chunky, good-quality body is fully jointed, and apart from being unusually large for this mould number, the doll is made of particularly pale bisque. The blond mohair wig and dress and shoes are original to the doll. This mould number was marketed by Kämmer & Reinhardt under the names Elsa and Walter, depending on whether it was dressed as a girl or a boy.

This Kämmer & Reinhardt doll is incised with the mark K. [star] R. *109 54*; it is 21¼in (54cm) tall. The red sailor dress and mousey blond wig are original to the doll, which was marketed under the name Elise. The blue eyes are painted, and the mouth is closed. The rather thick, stocky body is pink composition.

The shorter of these two German character dolls is one of Kämmer & Reinhardt's mould number *101* dolls, which was marketed as Marie and Peter. The doll bears the incised mark *K.* [star] *R. 101 39*, the *39* indicating height – i.e., 39cm (15½in). The eyes are glass. The fine quality body is jointed, and the regional costume is original to the doll.

The right-hand doll, also wearing its original regional dress, is an extremely rare Simon & Halbig doll. Incised *Simon & Halbig 1308*, the original shop label is still on the sole of one foot. The doll's mouth is closed and the body is that of an older child or young woman. The blue glass eyes are fixed, and the completely bald bisque head is covered by the original wig, which is braided and piled on top of the head. The doll is 17in (43cm) tall.

Peter

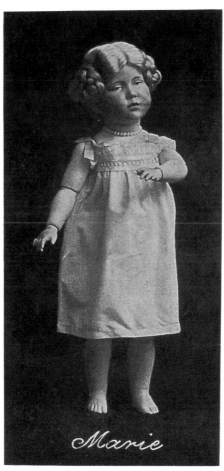

Marie

The model for the heads of Peter and Marie was produced for Kämmer & Reinhardt by the same Berlin artist who had made the very first baby dolls' head.

This large Kämmer & Reinhardt toddler doll bears the incised mark *K.* [star] *R. Simon & Halbig 116 50*. The doll is actually taller than the 50cm suggested by the mark on its head; it would have been 50cm (19½in) tall had the head been on a baby-style body, but the original side hip jointed toddler body used gives the doll an overall height of 55cm (21½in). It is very unusual to find this mould number with a closed-crown head. The doll's period North American Indian clothes resemble a child's play costume rather than authentic Indian dress. The felt rabbit with wooden wheels was made by Steiff.

The two dolls in Scottish dress were both manufactured by Kämmer & Reinhardt. The left-hand doll is incised *K.* [star] *R. 112 43*, and it is 17in (43cm) tall. The mouth is open/closed with two moulded upper teeth, and the blue eyes are painted. This doll was marketed as Walter (see also page 87).

The right-hand doll is incised *K.* [star] *R. 101 49*; it is 19¼in (49cm) tall. The doll was marketed as Peter when dressed as a boy as here, and as Marie when dressed as a girl.

This character doll is among the rarest of Kämmer & Reinhardt's early series. The head bears the incised mark *K*. [star] *R. 103 59*; the doll is 23in (59cm) tall. The painted blue eyes are side-glancing, and the doll has a rather pensive expression. The original blond mohair wig has the typical ram's horn braids coiled over the ears. This doll represents an older as opposed to a young child.

Among the rarest of all German character dolls, illustrated here is one of Kämmer & Reinhardt's mould number *104* dolls bearing the incised mark *K.* [star] *R. 104.* There is no centimetre size incised on the back of the doll's neck, and it is possible that this doll was a prototype for the mould and was not produced in any quantity. In 1909, when Kämmer & Reinhardt introduced its character series, the company produced 14 moulds, probably marketing only those that found favour with the toy distributors when they were exhibited at the Leipzig Toy Fair in 1909. Mould number *104* must have been one of the models that was not popular, and it was not manufactured for mass consumption. It is, however, an exquisitely modelled doll, with an open/closed mouth, deep dimples, a square chin and a mischievous look – not a handsome doll, but one that required craftsmanship to execute. It has far more detailed modelling than is found on other, more popular mould numbers such as *101, 109* and *114.*

Both of these dolls have painted eyes. On the left is a Kämmer & Reinhardt mould number *102*. The doll is 21¾in (54cm) tall and has a good quality, pink composition jointed body. The features and hair are delicately moulded, and the doll may well be modelled on the same child as Kämmer & Reinhardt's mould number *107* doll, which was marketed under the name Carl (see also opposite and page 88).

The right-hand doll is incised *Simon & Halbig 150 no. 2*. It is 19in (48cm) tall, and the jointed composition body is very good quality.

The left-hand doll was marketed by Kämmer & Reinhardt as Carl (see opposite and page 88). The mark *K. [star] R. 107 29* is incised on its head; it is 11½in (29cm) tall. The fully jointed composition body is of excellent quality, and the doll is wearing its original Tyrolean costume and *lederhosen.*

The lady doll on the right of the illustration bears the incised mark *1303 S. & H.* and the incised figure *6,* which indicates head size; also on the back of the head are the words *Wimpern Geschütz* printed in red. The doll, which is 15½in (39cm) tall is wearing an original brown velvet and black satin walking dress typical of the Edwardian period and a wide-brimmed straw hat lined with red silk. The doll's "sleeping" eyes are brown glass, and the deeply modelled face has a closed mouth with reddish-brown lips; the ears are pierced.

The girl doll and toddler were both manufactured by Kämmer & Reinhardt. The girl doll, which is 20½in (52cm) tall, bears the incised mark *K. [star] R. Simon & Halbig 117* on its head. At the base of the neck the figure *50* is incised. Usually an incised number at the base of the neck of a Kämmer & Reinhardt doll indicates the doll's size – in this instance 50cm. However, similar heads were sometimes mounted on bodies for which they had not originally been intended, and in this case the number should be ignored. The brown glass eyes move, and the mouth is closed;

the jointed body is composition.

The toddler bears on its head the incised mark *K. [star] R. S. & H. 115/A* and on its neck the figure *42* to indicate its size; the doll is 16½in (42cm) tall. The jointed composition body has side hip joints. (A toddler doll is one with the proportions of a child who has just learned to walk; a baby doll usually has bent limbs and can sit but not stand.) The doll's blue glass eyes move, and the mouth is closed. Kämmer & Reinhardt produced this particular model from 1911 to 1927.

Standing 18in (46cm) tall, this Kämmer & Reinhardt doll bears the incised mark *K. [star] R. 112*. The moving eyes are of brown glass, and two moulded teeth may be seen in the open/closed mouth. The jointed body is composition. The doll illustrated, with its open crown, wig and glass eyes, is the rarest version of this model; the doll was manufactured also with painted eyes, and another version has a solid crown and "flocked" hair. Kämmer & Reinhardt produced this doll both as a boy, when it was called Walter, and as a girl, when it was called Elsa (see also pages 76 and 81).

The straw hat bears a printed label showing a crest and the manufacturer's name and address.

The doll dressed in doctor's clothes was manufactured by Kämmer & Reinhardt and marketed under the name Carl (see pages 84 and 85); when the doll was dressed in this way, it was sold with a range of miniature medical instruments. The mark *K. [star] R. 107* is incised on the doll's head, which has painted blue eyes and a closed mouth. The jointed body is composition, and the doll is 21½in (55cm) tall.

The doll wearing its original nurse's uniform is unmarked. The brown eyes are intaglio, and the mouth is closed. The doll is 23in (59cm) tall and has a jointed composition adult woman's body.

In the bed is a doll bearing the incised mark *150 S. & H.* It has brown painted eyes, a closed mouth and a jointed composition body; it is 14in (36cm) tall.

The factory name for this Kämmer & Reinhardt girl doll was Gretchen. It is incised *K. [star] R. 114 64* and is 25in (64cm) tall. The blue glass eyes move and the mouth is closed. The fully jointed composition body is of a type often found on Kämmer & Reinhardt dolls. The version of this mould number that has glass eyes, as seen here, is rarer than the ones with painted eyes.

The boy doll, generally known as Hans, bears the incised mark *K. [star] R. 114 64*, and it is 25in (64cm) tall. The doll's brown eyes are painted, and its mouth is closed. Like Gretchen, it has a fully jointed composition body.

Kämmer & Reinhardt's mould numbers *114, 115* and *117* are the most sought-after of all that company's character dolls.

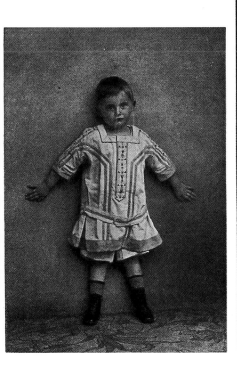

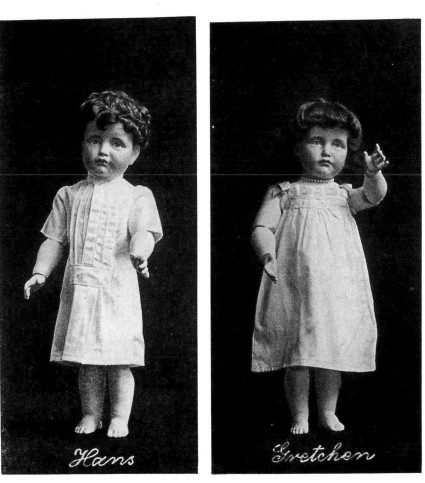

Reinhardt's grandson (left) was
the model for Hans and Gretchen,
the company's great success of
1910.

Probably made by Kestner, the closed-mouth, glass-eyed doll bears only the incised number *128*. The doll is 21in (53cm) tall, and the good quality, jointed body is of composition. The raised eyebrows are enamelled in the manner often found on Simon & Halbig dolls; however, the high forehead and the very small open crown at the rear of the head are more typical of character dolls produced by such companies as Kley & Hahn or Catterfelder Puppenfabrik. The white dress and straw hat seen here are contemporary with the doll.

This is an unusually large example of a painted-eye Kestner – it is $22\frac{3}{4}$in (58cm) tall – and it bears the incised mark *K. Made in Germany 14 208* on the back of its head. The doll has an excellent quality, fully jointed body. The human hair wig is original to the doll, and the red, black and green check dress is contemporary with it.

These three Kestner dolls with painted eyes are all 18in (46cm) tall. To the left of the group is a mould *180* doll with an open/closed mouth, moulded upper teeth and painted blue eyes. The light brown mohair wig with coiled braids above the ears is original to the doll, as is its white cotton and lace dress. The doll was originally part of a Kestner boxed set.

The girl doll with the red bow in its hair at the front of the group is a mould number *186*; it has an open/closed mouth and brown painted eyes. The boy doll is a mould number *187*; it has a closed mouth. Originally these two dolls' heads were part of a boxed set with a glass-eyed, open-mouth doll, but they have since been put on jointed bodies and dressed in appropriate clothes of the period. The wigs are original to the heads.

The Kestner doll on the left of the illustration is $15\frac{3}{4}$in (40cm) tall and bears the incised number *189*. The "smiling" mouth is closed, and the "sleeping" eyes are blue glass, while on the back of the good quality jointed pink composition body is the original toyshop label: "G.A. Schwartz & Company, Philadelphia." The blond mohair wig, coiled in braids above the ears, is original to the doll.

The right-hand doll, although unmarked, is probably by Kestner. In the open mouth may be seen two square upper teeth and one square lower tooth. The "sleeping" eyes are grey, and the blond mohair wig is original to the doll. The good quality body, with unjointed wrists, is typical of early Kestner dolls. The doll is 11in (28cm) tall.

Manufactured *c.*1910 by the
Waltershausen company J.D. Kestner,
this doll bears on its head the incised
number *178*. The blue glass eyes move,
but it is more usual to find this doll
with painted eyes. The mouth is
open/closed, and the jointed body is
composition. The doll is 11½in (29cm)
tall.

This oriental-looking baby doll by
Kestner bears the incised mark *243
J.D.K. Germany*, and the dress still has
a Kestner label, visible under the doll's
chin, attached to it. Two teeth may be
seen in the open mouth, and the brown
glass eyes move. The doll, which is
$13\frac{1}{2}$in (34cm) tall, has a five-piece
composition body with bent limbs.

Made *c.*1912, this Kestner oriental doll
is from the company's *150* series. The
black hair is painted, and the eyes are
glass. The mouth is open. The five-
piece, jointed baby body with bent
limbs is composition.

The doll in the white broderie anglaise dress and hat bears the incised mark *Th* (or) *Fl* [in script] *Made in Germany 12 J.D.K. 241*. The glass eyes are brown and the open mouth has four teeth.

The doll is 23in (59cm) tall. Printed in red on the jointed composition body is the word *Germany* [in an oblong] above the number *4*. The doll is particularly sought after by American collectors.

Several doll manufacturers produced dolls based on Wilhelm Busch's comic characters Max and Moritz. Illustrated here are versions by Kämmer & Reinhardt and by J.D. Kestner. The larger dolls are by Kämmer & Reinhardt. Max, with black hair and moulded black shoes, is marked *K. [star] R. 123*; Moritz, with red hair and shoes, is marked *K. [star] R. 124*. Both

dolls are 16in (41cm) tall. The wigs are made of heavily starched, dyed flax, and the dolls' brown, flirty eyes are controlled by a wire mechanism. The fully jointed composition bodies have pointed fingers. Both dolls are extremely rare.

The smaller, all-bisque versions of Max and Moritz were made by the Waltershausen firm of J.D. Kestner.

Jointed at elbows and hips, they also have pointed fingers. Although the dolls illustrated here have moulded and painted clothes, another all-bisque version has commercial cloth garments instead of moulded ones.

A Moritz doll was manufactured also by the American firm Albert Schoenhut & Co. of Philadelphia from 1907.

The doll representing an old lady bears the indistinct incised mark *Geselel Gesch* [in script]. This probably stands for *Gesetlich Geschützt*, which indicates that the doll was registered or patented in Germany. The fixed glass eyes are brown, and the mouth is closed. The jointed body is composition, and the doll stands 15 in (38cm) tall.

The right-hand doll, which was probably manufactured by Kestner, is unmarked. It has painted eyes, a closed mouth and moulded hair. The jointed composition body has fixed wrists. The factory name for the doll was Max, one of a pair of dolls based on the cartoon characters Max and Moritz (see opposite).

The left- and right-hand dolls illustrated here are bisque-headed bonnet dolls. The right-hand doll, a Gebrüder Heubach mould number *79 59*, bears the incised square Heubach symbol, size number *6* and the word *Germany*. The blue intaglio eyes are deeply cut and glance to the right. The lacy pink bonnet and three curls of hair on the forehead are moulded. The mouth is open/closed, and there is a deep dimple in the lower lip while two moulded teeth may be seen on the upper lip. The long-legged jointed body is composition, and the doll is $17\frac{1}{2}$ in (45 cm) tall. The dress is original to the doll.

The left-hand doll was manufactured by J.D. Kestner, and the incised letters *J.D.K.* may be seen at the back of the neck. The doll is $13\frac{3}{4}$ in (35 cm) tall and has a toddler-style composition body with side hip joints. The blue and white bonnet and locks

of hair escaping from under the bonnet
onto the forehead and above the ears
are moulded. The doll is very rare and,
although it does not bear a mould
number, is very similar to Kestner's
model *247*.

The doll in the centre is a version of
Armand Marseille's *Fany* (see page

106) but with moulded hair. The doll,
which is 19½in (50cm) tall, has blue
glass "sleeping" eyes and a closed
mouth. The body is the same as the
wooden version. The mould number is
2307231, but the incised marks are *Fany*
[in script] *230 A. 7 M*.

Both the dolls illustrated here were manufactured by the Thüringian company Kley & Hahn. Kley & Hahn did not have its own porcelain factory, and it is now believed that the majority of its character dolls were produced either by the porcelain firm Hertel, Schwab & Co. or by the Ohrdruf-based Bähr & Pröschild. The left-hand doll, which is 28in (46cm) tall, bears the incised mark *K. & H.* [in a banner] *526*. The eyes and winged eyebrows are painted, and the mouth is closed. The blond mohair wig is probably original to the doll, and the blue sailor dress is contemporary with it.

The right-hand doll, which is 20½in (52cm) tall, is incised *K. & H.* [in a banner] *546*. The eyes are glass, and the mouth is closed. Unlike most character dolls of this period, the ears are pierced. Both wig and dress are original to the doll.

The doll's head bears the incised mark *A. Ellar M. 355/3K* and was manufactured by Armand Marseille. Although the doll is now bald, there is a small hole in the top of its head through which a tuft of hair once protruded. The "sleeping" eyes are of blue glass, and the mouth is closed. The doll is 12½in (32cm) tall, and the five-piece composition body has bent limbs.

The left-hand doll, which was manufactured by Armand Marseille, bears the incised mark *Fany* [in script] *231 A.7 M.* The doll's mouth is closed, and the "sleeping" eyes are glass. The rather fat toddler body has joints at shoulders, elbows, hips and knees but not at the wrists, and it does not have the side hip joints typical of many toddler-style dolls. The doll is 19½in (50cm) tall.

The right-hand doll, which is very similar to the Armand Marseille doll, was in fact manufactured by Kämmer & Reinhardt. It bears the incised mark *K.* [star] *R. Simon & Halbig 115/A 42* and is one of the company's *115A* mould number dolls. The doll is 16½in (42cm) tall, the incised number *42* indicating height. The body is more typical of the toddler-style, having side hip joints and jointed wrists. The facial features of both dolls resemble those of early Käthe Kruse cloth dolls.

Bearing the incised mark *700 2/0*, this doll has been attributed to Armand Marseille. The moving eyes are brown, and the eyebrows are painted in one stroke. The doll's mouth is closed. The five-piece composition body has bent limbs, and the doll is 13½in (34cm) tall.

Both these googly-eyed dolls are attributed to Armand Marseille. The right-hand doll bears the incised mark *240 0*, and it has fixed, blue glass eyes. The doll's mouth is closed, and the five-piece toddler body is of composition. The doll is $10\frac{1}{2}$in (27cm) tall. The closed-crown version of this doll is rarer than the open-crown version.

The left-hand doll, which is $11\frac{1}{2}$in (29cm) tall, bears the incised mark *241 0*. The mouth is closed, but the brown glass eyes, which look sideways, move up and down. The fully jointed composition body has side hip joints, and the open-crown head is covered by a wig.

LEFT

This doll, which has painted blue eyes and a closed mouth, bears the incised mark *A. 4 M*. The composition body, which is jointed but with fixed wrists, is typically German in style, and the all original doll is 16in (41cm) tall.

The all-bisque baby doll in the box has joints at the shoulders only. The blue eyes are painted, and the bonnet is moulded. The doll is 9in (23cm) tall.

This flange-necked doll bears on its head the incised words *Copyright Grace C. Rockwell Germany*. The body is cloth, but the arms and legs are made of American composition, which tends to crack much more readily than its German equivalent. The doll has blue glass eyes and a closed mouth. It stands 15in (38cm) tall.

Incised on the back of this doll's head are the words *Copr by Grace C. Rockwell Germany*. Grace Corry Rockwell was an American who, in the 1920s, designed both bisque-head and composition character dolls. The doll illustrated here is 17in (43cm) tall and has a cloth body with composition arms and legs, blue glass eyes, a closed mouth and moulded hair.

Below the incised mark *B.P.5* on the head of this intaglio-eyed doll is a stamp that reads *S. & Co.* [in a circle]. Although the initials B.P. are widely thought to stand for the porcelain factory of Bähr & Pröschild, the doll's head is uncharacteristic of the type of porcelain produced by that company. It is more likely that the head, at least, was made by Armand Marseille for the relatively obscure doll manufacturer Swaine & Co., Hüttensteinach, Thüringia. The doll is wearing its original regional costume.

This black fired-in-bisque doll has moving glass eyes. It is incised *SQ* [intertwined] *252* for the Boilstädt company Schützmeister & Quendt, a porcelain manufacturer producing bisque dolls and dolls' heads and distributed by Gebrüder Bing. The doll has a five-piece, bent-limb baby body, an open-crown head and a curly black caracul wig. It is 16in (41cm) tall and is wearing its original factory clothes.

Both the Simon & Halbig dolls illustrated here bear the incised mark *S.H. 151*, but the taller doll, which is 26¾in (68cm) tall, has the incised number *4* to indicate size, while the girl doll, which is 23in (59cm) tall, bears the incised number *3*. Both dolls have good quality, jointed composition bodies, and both are wearing their original costumes. The boy doll has its original light brown mohair wig; the girl doll's wig is of curly human hair.

This doll, which dates from the early 1900s, is probably earlier than many of the dolls illustrated in this book. It bears the incised mark *Simon & Halbig S. & H. 1279 13*, the *13* indicating head size. The doll is 26¾in (68cm) tall. The blond mohair wig is original to the doll, which has arched painted eyebrows with deep furrows, and an open mouth with shading in the centre of the lower lip and four moulded teeth. Another version of this doll has only two moulded teeth and lacks the rather exaggerated facial modelling. The good quality, yellow jointed body was probably made by Heinrich Handwerck of Waltershausen.

The doll to the left of the illustration is a black fired-in-bisque character doll incised *1358 Simon & Halbig S. & H. 8*, the *8* indicating head size. The doll is 21 in (53 cm) tall. The red of the lips is also fired in the bisque, and moulded teeth are visible in the open mouth. The "sleeping" eyes are of brown glass, and the black jointed body is composition. Both the black wig and the red and white striped shift are original to the doll.

The right-hand doll is also a black fired-in-bisque character, but the brown eyes are intaglio. Two moulded lower teeth may be seen in the open/closed mouth, and the jointed body is of brown composition. The doll is incised *R. A.* for the firm Recknagel of Alexandrienthal, and this is probably one of the rarest of all black bisque character dolls ever made.

This Simon & Halbig doll bears the incised mark *150 S. & H. 3*. The painted eyes are blue, and the mouth is closed. The doll's jointed body is of composition, and the doll stands 24in (61cm) tall. Founded in Gräfenhain, Thüringia, in 1869 to produce porcelain, Simon & Halbig quickly established a reputation for producing dolls' heads of the highest quality. The company merged with Kämmer & Reinhardt in 1920 after having supplied the Waltershausen firm with heads for its dolls for several years.

This Simon & Halbig lady doll, which is from the company's *100* series, bears the incised mark *S. & H. 1527*. The blue eyes are painted, and the mouth is closed. The fully jointed, lady-style body is made of composition. The doll is 20in (51cm) tall.

LEFT
One of the rarest of all Simon & Halbig character dolls, this doll bears the incised mark *1388 Germany Simon & Halbig 12*. The brown glass eyes move, and there are modelled teeth in the open/closed mouth. The body, which is composition, is jointed, and the doll stands 25in (64cm) tall.

The right-hand doll is incised with the mark *Simon & Halbig SH IV*. The eyes are glass, and the mouth is closed; the ears are pierced. The good quality composition body is jointed. The doll's eyebrows are painted in the manner typical of early glass-eyed Kämmer & Reinhardt dolls. The brown mohair wig is pulled to the top of the head, where it is tied in a knot with a cap fitting over the knot and fastened with ribbons under the doll's chin. The original costume is from the Hessian region of Germany.

The left-hand doll, which was manufactured by Armand Marseille, bears the incised mark *Germany 550 A. 4 M. D.R.G.M.* The doll's mouth is closed, and the "sleeping" eyes are brown glass. The wig is original to the doll as is the traditional costume, which probably represents a region of Poland.

LEFT
This Simon & Halbig doll, which is incised *1305 S. & H. 8½*, has a jointed, lady-type German body and is 20in (51cm) tall. The brown glass eyes move, and the mouth is open/closed. The "screaming" baby doll, which has tiny glass eyes and an open/closed mouth, is incised *255 2 O.I.C.* The doll, which is 12in (30cm) tall and has a cloth body with composition hands, was made by Kestner.

The dolls illustrated here were manufactured, from left to right, by Armand Marseille, Catterfelder Puppenfabrik and Simon & Halbig.

The Armand Marseille doll, which bears the incised mark *A. 4 M.*, has blue intaglio eyes and a closed mouth. The head is of an excellent quality "oily" bisque, the body is fully jointed, and the doll stands 17in (43cm) tall. The costume is original to the doll, which is wearing a wig of human hair coiled in braids over the ears. This is one of several dolls in a character series by Armand Marseille that bears no mould number.

The doll in the centre is incised *C.P.* for Catterfelder Puppenfabrik of Catterfeld, Thüringia, a company that was established in 1906 and that specialized in the production of bisque-head composition dolls. The jointed body of the doll seen here is of good quality. The mouth is closed, the painted eyes are blue, and the eyebrows have been painted in one stroke. The wig is mohair. The doll, which is wearing its original pink costume and white pinafore, is 15½in (39cm) tall.

The Simon & Halbig doll in the period sailor suit bears the incised mark *S. & H. 153*. The hair is deeply sculpted. The doll is 17in (43cm) tall and is often referred to as "Little Duke" by collectors.

On the left of this illustration is a Kley & Hahn character doll incised *K. & H.* [within a banner] *520*. This particular doll has an open-crown head covered by a wig, but dolls with the same mould number are found also with bald, closed-dome heads. The brown painted eyes are surmounted by winged eyebrows; the "smiling" mouth is closed; and the doll has two dimples. The doll, which stands $24\frac{1}{2}$in (62cm) tall, is wearing the original evening dress and top hat.

The right-hand doll, which is 24in (61cm) tall, is an extremely rare Simon & Halbig doll incised *1398 Simon & Halbig*. As early as 1890, Simon & Halbig had taken out a patent on "flirty" eyes – that is, eyes that could move from side to side – but not only do this doll's glass eyes move, the doll has also a "walking" body, which means that as it walks, the head turns from side to side, making the eyes move. The eyelashes are of brown silk, and there is a slight opening between the teeth and lower lip. The doll's period dress is from the German region of Hesse.

Although this doll is almost certainly German and its head is incised with the letter *S*, it cannot positively be identified as having been manufactured by Simon & Halbig. This is a rare example of a character doll representing not only a man, but also an old man with wrinkles and grey eyebrows. The doll illustrated, dressed in the style known as "Uncle Sam", is especially rare: this type of doll is usually smaller than the doll shown, which is 29in (74cm) tall. The head is incised with the mark *S.15*. The blue glass eyes are fixed, and the mouth is closed. The jointed body is composition and wood.

Known to most doll collectors as "pouty", this glass-eyed character doll is incised *S.F.B.J. 2525 11 Paris*. The S.F.B.J. (*Société Française de Fabrication des Bébés et Jouets*) was a syndicate formed in 1899 by Fleischmann & Bloedel, Pintel & Godchaux, Genty, Girard, Remignard, Gobert, the porcelain manufacturer Gaultier, and Jumeau to counter the threat from German doll manufacturers. The doll seen here has a French toddler-style body with side hip joints. The bat, Eric, is by Steiff.

This pair of black fired-in-bisque character dolls, both incised *S.F.B.J. 227* and both 19¼in (49cm) tall, are unusual in that this particular mould number is more commonly found on smaller, white bisque dolls. Dressed in their original African-style clothing, these dolls are quite exceptional. The boy doll on the right has black "flocked" hair topped by a fez; the girl doll has a wig representing mud-soaked braids with gold beading and wrapped in a turban.

The "smiling" toddler doll was probably manufactured by the S.F.B.J., for although the doll's head is unmarked, the composition body was made by the syndicate. The blue glass eyes are fixed, and the open/closed mouth has a moulded tongue. The doll stands 27in (69cm) tall.

The baby doll bears the incised mark *1924 E. Horsman & Co. Made in Germany 11/G.* The open-crown head is covered by a blond wig, and the five-piece baby body has bent limbs.

Although its head is unmarked, this
doll too was probably manufactured
by the S.F.B.J., which produced the
jointed wood and composition body.
The black, pupil-less eyes are of glass
and are fixed, and the open/closed
mouth has six moulded teeth. The doll
is 32in (81cm) tall.

The moulded head of this French doll bears the incised mark *S.F.B.J. 233 Paris 4*. The fixed glass eyes are blue, and the open/closed mouth has both upper and lower moulded teeth. The S.F.B.J. five-piece body has bent limbs, and the doll stands 13 in (33 cm) tall.

Incised *S.F.B.J. 262*, this doll has blue glass eyes and an open mouth with two moulded teeth. The doll is 22 in (56 cm) tall and has a jointed wood and composition body.

This extremely rare fashion doll, although unmarked, was probably made by Jules Nicholas Steiner of Paris, an imaginative and innovative doll manufacturer, who took out patents not only for talking and walking dolls, but also for artificial eyes, for a type of moulded composition for dolls' bodies and for unbreakable bisque and porcelain to be used for dolls' heads. The doll seen here has a swivel head, ten teeth in two rows, brown paperweight eyes and pierced ears. The body is of brown kid, and the Ethiopian costume is original to the doll.

LEFT
Possibly made by the company that made "Uncle Sam" (see page 124), this shoulder-head doll with fixed neck is unmarked except for *N 1* incised on the shoulder-plate. The brown glass eyes are fixed, and moulded teeth are visible in the open/closed mouth. The legs and arms are composition although the body is cloth. The doll stands 13in (33cm) tall.

This Campbell Kid, with its moulded red hair, is 16½in (42cm) tall. Its side-glancing blue glass eyes move up and down, and its mouth is closed. The jointed composition body has side hip joints. Campbell Kid dolls first appeared in 1900, designed for the Joseph Campbell Company to promote its soup, and the earliest dolls were probably produced by the New York toy and games manufacturer E.I. Horsman & Co.

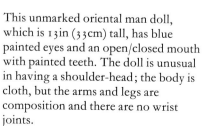

This unmarked oriental man doll, which is 13in (33cm) tall, has blue painted eyes and an open/closed mouth with painted teeth. The doll is unusual in having a shoulder-head; the body is cloth, but the arms and legs are composition and there are no wrist joints.

The black, fully jointed body of this doll is French in style, but the doll itself is unmarked and no maker can be identified. The amber glass eyes are fixed, and the mouth is open/closed. The black of the head is fired-in-bisque: that is, the head was painted black after the initial firing of the bisque and then re-fired at a lower temperature to set the colour. The doll is 17in (43cm) tall.

In addition to the employees working either at Kämmer & Reinhardt's Waltershausen factory itself or at the nearby Heinrich Handwerck factory, which Kämmer & Reinhardt had bought in 1902, many local families worked at home to provide doll parts. Three generations of the same family may be seen here. They were all engaged in the manufacture of dolls' bodies, and it is known the dolls' limbs were also moulded by home-based workers.

The skilled task of blowing glass eyes was also carried out by workers operating from home. On the table in front of the couple seen here are the bundles of coloured glass, while in the foreground and in the man's left hand are clearly visible the gas jets in which the glass was heated until it became malleable. Producing closely matched pairs of eyes was difficult and required both steady hands and good eyesight.

Glossary

Applied ears: the term used to describe ears made in separate moulds and attached to the doll's head before the first firing of the bisque rather than being integral features of the doll's head.

Armature: the internal framework of wire, metal or wood that is used to assist in maintaining a doll's posture.

Articulated: the term used to describe a doll with joints allowing the various limbs to move.

Automaton (pl. **automata**): a figure or toy that has some form of movement activated by mechanical means.

Bathing doll: see Frozen Charlotte.

Bisque (sometimes known also as biscuit): a ceramic material that can be poured or pressed into a mould before being fired at a high temperature. Bisque dolls' heads were generally painted before being fired for a second time at a lower temperature. It has a matt, unglazed surface.

Blown glass eyes: dolls' eyes that are hollow globes of glass.

Breveté (French): patented; abbreviated to *Bte*.

Celluloid: the first plastic, invented in America in 1869 by the Hyatt brothers, came to replace wax, papier mâché and bisque in the manufacture of dolls' heads and bodies. Highly flammable, and for this reason later not used for toys and dolls, it was also known as biskoline, pyroxyline, miblu and cellowach.

Composition: the name given to a number of substances (including papier mâché) that were used to make dolls' bodies. It was usually composed of wood pulp or sawdust and an adhesive of some kind.

Déposé (French) or **Deponiert** (German): often abbreviated to *Dep* or *D.E.P.* and found incised on the bisque shoulder-plate or head of a doll to indicate that the manufacturer's trademark or patent had been registered.

D.R.G.M. (Deutsches Reichsgebrauchsmuster): the initials used, from 1909, to indicate that a design or patent was registered in Germany.

Fired-in-bisque: a term used to describe the process by which the tints used to colour a doll's head were painted on the bisque after the first, but before the second, firing. The second firing, at a lower temperature than the first, sets the paint.

Frozen Charlotte: the name given in the United States to a doll made in one piece, with head, body, arms and legs moulded together. Such dolls are also known as bathing babies (or dolls), pillar dolls and solid chinas.

Gesetzlich geschützt (German): patented; abbreviated to *Ges. Gesch*.

Googly eyes: side-glancing eyes, either fixed or painted; such eyes are also known as "roguish" eyes. The term "googly" is used to refer to dolls with this type of eye.

Gutta-percha: a tough, greyish-black substance, obtained from the latex of Malaysian trees. It resembles rubber but tends to become somewhat brittle with age. It was used in the 1880s to make dolls' heads and bodies.

Incised marks: marks, generally in the form of numbers or letter, that are incised into the bisque of a doll's head or shoulder-plate, sometimes both. Bisque heads and shoulder-plates were generally marked by the factory that produced them; only the largest doll making companies could afford their own porcelain works and, therefore, dolls that were unique to themselves.

Intaglio eyes: painted eyes in which the details of pupil and iris have been engraved.

Jointed body: an alternative term for articulated body (*q.v.*).

Moulded teeth: the term used to describe teeth that have been moulded in one with the doll's head and not applied separately in a strip.

Open/closed mouth: the term used to describe dolls in which the lips appear to be parted although there is, in fact, no mouth opening. A fine white line is often painted between the lips.

Papier mâché: a paper pulp, combined with a whitening agent and a suitable glue, that was used for the manufacture of dolls' heads and bodies in the early 19th century. At the end of the century, a new type of papier mâché, which could be poured into a mould rather than having to be pressure moulded, was developed. It was stronger and more durable than the earlier mixture.

Pate: the crown of the head. The word is also used to describe the piece of cork or cardboard that was used to cover the hole made in the crown of some dolls' heads and to which the wigs were attached.

S.F.B.J. (Société Française de Fabrication de Bébés et Jouets): a syndicate formed in 1899 by Fleischmann & Bloedel, Pintel & Godchaux, Genty, Girard, Remignard, Gobert, Jumeau, Bru and the porcelain manufacturer Gaultier to counter the threat posed to the French doll making industry by German doll manufacturers.

S.G.D.G (Sans Garantie du Gouvernement): initials found on French dolls signifying that a patent or trademark had not yet been registered – literally, that it had not yet been guaranteed by the French government.

Snow Baby: a small, all-bisque doll, the painted clothes of which look as if they are covered with snow, an effect achieved by covering the unfired porcelain with a coarse-grained slip.

Täufling (German): the term used to describe a baby doll dressed in a shift or christening clothes.

Toddler body: a doll's body with a fat torso and side hip joints, with either straight or jointed legs; it has the shape of a walking infant as distinct from the bent-limb dolls representing babies.

Wax over: the term applied to dolls that are made from a base substance, either composition or papier mâché, that is, dipped into, or painted with, molten wax.

Wimpern (German): eyebrows.

Bibliography

Readers are advised that, for general information about doll making and manufacturers, the three following books should be consulted. All contain extensive bibliographies, listing books, articles, directories, catalogues and some exhibition sources.

Cieslik, Jürgen and Marianne, *German Doll Encyclopedia, 1800–1939*, Hobby House Press Inc., Maryland, 1985; White Mouse Publications, London, 1985

Coleman, Dorothy S., Elizabeth A. and Evelyn J., *The Collector's Encyclopedia of Dolls*, volume I, Crown Publishers Inc., New York, 1968; Robert Hale Ltd, London, 1970

Coleman, Dorothy S., Elizabeth A. and Evelyn J., *The Collector's Encyclopedia of Dolls*, volume II, Crown Publishers Inc., New York, 1986; Robert Hale Ltd, London, 1987

For information on individual manufacturers, the following titles are recommended.

Anka, G. and Gauder U., *An Example of Dolls Made in Waltershausen by König & Wernicke*, Ritter, Stuttgart, 1976

Buchholz, Shirley, *A Century of Celluloid Dolls*, Hobby House Press Inc., Maryland, 1983

Coleman, Dorothy S. (ed.), *My Darling Dolls* (reprint of Kämmer & Reinhardt 1927 catalogue), Pyne Press, 1972

Cooper, Marlow, *Doll Home Library Series*, volume I, *S.F.B.J. French Characters*, privately published, 1969

Davies, Nina S., *The Jumeau Doll Story*, Hobby House Press Inc., Maryland, 1969

Ellenburg, M. Kelly, *Effanbee: The Dolls with the Golden Hearts*, Trojan Press, 1973

Foulke, Jan, *Focusing on . . . Effanbee Composition Dolls*, Hobby House Press Inc., Maryland, 1978

Foulke, Jan, *Focusing on . . . Gebrüder Heubach Dolls*, Hobby House Press Inc., Maryland, 1980

Foulke, Jan, *Kestner: King of Doll Makers*, Hobby House Press Inc., Maryland, 1982

Foulke, Jan, *Simon & Halbig Dolls: The Artful Aspect*, Hobby House Press Inc., Maryland, 1984

Guthrie, D. L. and Haley, M. T., *A Portfolio of Armand Marseille Dolls*, The Fine Print, 1981

King, Constance Eileen, *Jumeau: Prince of Dollmakers*, Hobby House Press Inc., Maryland, 1983

MacDowell, R. and K., *The Collector's Digest of German Character Dolls*, Hobby House Press Inc., Maryland, 1981

Richter, Lydia, *Puppen Album (Deutsche Porzellanpuppen; Französische Porzellanpuppen; Käthe-Kruse-Puppen; Charakterpuppen; and Orientalen – Negerpuppen und Exoten)*, Laterna Magica, Munich, 1980–2

Scherf, H., *Thüringer Porzellan*, Ebeling, 1980

Schoonmaker, P. N., *Effanbee Dolls*, Hobby House Press Inc., Maryland, 1984

Tarnowska, Marce, *Fashion Dolls*, Hobby House Press Inc., Maryland, 1986; Souvenir Press, London, 1986

Theimer, François, *Si Huret M'Etait*, Polichinelle, 1980

Theimer, François, *Le Bébé Jumeau*, Polichinelle, 1985

Whitton, Margaret, *The Jumeau Doll*, Dover Publications, New York, 1980

Kämmer & Reinhardt's sample room, in which not only fully assembled and dressed dolls could be inspected, but also the full range of individual heads could be examined.

Acknowledgements

The author and publishers would like to take this opportunity to thank all those who have contributed to this book by allowing their dolls to be photographed and by providing invaluable information about them: Richard Wright, whose dolls are illustrated on pages 37, 41, 43, 44, 46, 47, 48, 49, 50, 51, 58, 59, 60, 61, 76, 77, 78, 80, 81, 82, 83, 84, 85, 92, 93, 94, 95, 100, 102, 103, 104, 106, 112, 113, 114, 115, 116, 121, 122, 123, 125, 129 (below), 130 and 131; Ralph Griffith and Elmer Bell, whose dolls are illustrated on pages 2, 6, 36 (above), 40, 42, 52, 53, 54, 56 (below), 62, 63, 64, 65, 66, 67, 68, 69, 70, 71, 72, 73, 74, 75, 101, 108, 111, 119, 120, 124, 127 (below), 128, 132 and 134 (above and below); Dorothy Hertig, whose dolls may be seen on pages 36 (below), 38, 55 (above and below), 56 (above), 87, 96, 97, 110 and 129 (above); Mary Lou Rubright, whose dolls are shown on pages 39, 45, 88, 89, 99, 117 and 118; Jeanette Fink, whose dolls are illustrated on pages 126 and 127 (above); and Maree Tarnowska, whose dolls are illustrated on pages 57, 86, 90, 98, 105, 107, 109 and 133.

In addition, special thanks are due to Richard Wright, who kindly made available a copy of the booklet produced in 1911 by Kämmer & Reinhardt to celebrate its first twenty-five years. Illustrations from this booklet are reproduced on pages 12, 13, 14, 15, 16, 17, 25, 26, 79, 91, 135, 136, 140 and 142.

The advice and assistance of Jane Coleman and Rick Flaxman are also gratefully acknowledged. Finally, the contribution of Charles Farrow, whose support, encouragement and advice have been unfailing, is, as ever, acknowledged with gratitude and affection.

While men were employed in every
other process of doll manufacture, it
appears that only women were
involved in the delicate work of
stitching the mohair wigs.

Index

Page references in *italics* are to illustrations or illustration captions